CAMBRIDGE CHECKPOINTS VCE

Fourth Edition

Specialist Mathematics Units 1 & 2

- Fully revised content matched to the study design
- Revision questions arranged by Area of Study
- Suggested solutions

Peter Flynn

Shaftesbury Road, Cambridge CB2 8EA, United Kingdom

One Liberty Plaza, 20th Floor, New York, NY 10006, USA

477 Williamstown Road, Port Melbourne, VIC 3207, Australia

314–321, 3rd Floor, Plot 3, Splendor Forum, Jasola District Centre, New Delhi – 110025, India

103 Penang Road, #05–06/07, Visioncrest Commercial, Singapore 238467

Cambridge University Press & Assessment is a department of the University of Cambridge.

We share the University's mission to contribute to society through the pursuit of education, learning and research at the highest international levels of excellence.

www.cambridge.org

First published 2023
20 19 18 17 16 15 14 13 12 11 10 9 8 7 6 5

Cover image © Getty Images / marcoventuriniautieri
Printed in Australia by Ligare Book Printers.

A catalogue record for this book is available from the National Library of Australia at www.nla.gov.au

ISBN 978-1-009-30955-4 Paperback

Additional resources for this publication at www.cambridge.edu.au/GO

Cambridge University Press & Assessment acknowledges the Aboriginal and Torres Strait Islander Peoples of this nation. We acknowledge the traditional custodians of the lands on which our company is located and where we conduct our business. We pay our respects to ancestors and Elders, past and present. Cambridge University Press & Assessment is committed to honouring Aboriginal and Torres Strait Islander Peoples' unique cultural and spiritual relationships to the land, waters and seas and their rich contribution to society.

Contents

Introduction

This book presents you with a wide cross-section of revision questions that are excellent for reviewing Specialist Mathematics Units 1 and 2 material before starting your examinations. And since success in your study of Mathematics at the Units 3 and 4 level relies on having a full understanding of the topics you study in Units 1 and 2 Courses, these revision questions are very suitable for preparing you for Specialist Mathematics Units 3 and 4. Note that the external examinations papers at the end of Units 3 and 4 Mathematics Courses contain some questions that can be completed by students studying Specialist Mathematics Units 1 and 2. Such questions make excellent revision material and are included here along with other questions written especially for this book.

The majority of questions are either in multiple-choice format or in short-answer format. It is very important that you work through both multiple-choice and short-answer questions. You must know your basic material as well as the combination of various topics and formats.

The material in the chapters in this book with titles starting with 'A' relate to topics covered in Specialist Mathematics Unit 1. The material in the chapters in this book with titles starting with 'B' relate to topics covered in Specialist Mathematics Unit 2.

The questions in this book have matching solutions at the back. Work through these answers only after you have completed questions to the best of your ability. In some questions, there may be more than one solution approach. It is always a good idea to look at methods for doing particular questions other than those you have been shown in the classroom. The answers given here were written by the author and in no way represent 'official' answers. Every attempt has been made to ensure their accuracy.

There are some good techniques for answering multiple-choice questions. In some cases, a process of elimination is the best path to follow. In other cases, a separate solution followed by a search for the correct answer is best. Sometimes a combination of both techniques is needed.

Be sure of two things:

- there is an answer to each question
- the wrong alternatives have been very cleverly worked out. Some traps are present!

Answer all written questions with care, formality and neatness. Explain your work clearly. If you see an expression like 'give exact answers', then use fractions and surds and show all of your working. If you see 'correct to 2 decimal places', then it really means 2 decimal places. If the question involves units, such as seconds, metres, kilograms and so on, make sure that your answers include the correct units also.

We hope that you find these questions challenging, satisfying and useful.

A1. Proof and number

Question 1

Of the following expressions, the one that is **not** a rational number is

A. 3.14159 **B.** $0.\dot{9}$ **C.** $\sqrt[3]{64}$ **D.** $\frac{\sqrt{3}}{\sqrt{12}}$ **E.** $6^{\frac{1}{2}}$

Question 2

If n is a positive integer, then $n(n+1)(n+2)(n+3)$ is always divisible by

A. 11 **B.** 12 **C.** 13 **D.** 14 **E.** 15

Question 3

To rationalise the denominator of $\frac{\sqrt{2}-1}{\sqrt{2}+1}$, you would multiply the expression by

A. $\sqrt{2}-1$ **B.** $\frac{1}{\sqrt{2}-1}$ **C.** $\frac{1}{\sqrt{2}+1}$ **D.** $\frac{\sqrt{2}+1}{\sqrt{2}+1}$ **E.** $\frac{\sqrt{2}-1}{\sqrt{2}-1}$

Question 4

The natural number n is a perfect square greater than 1. Which one of the following **cannot** be a perfect square for any value of n?

A. $\sqrt{n}-1$ **B.** $2\sqrt{n}$ **C.** $n-1$ **D.** n^2-2n+1 **E.** $n^2-2\sqrt{n}+1$

Question 5

Let $U=\{1, 2, 3, 4, 5, 6, 7, 8, 9\}$, $A=\{1, 3, 5, 7\}$, $B=\{1, 2, 3, 4\}$ and $C=\{6, 7, 8\}$.

Find each of the following:

a. $A \cup B$

b. $A \cap C$

c. $A \cap (B \cup C)$

d. $(A \cap B) \cup (A \cap C)$

e. $(A \cup B)'$

f. $A' \cap B'$

Question 6

a. Find the power set, $P(A)$, for the set $A=\{2, 4, 6\}$.

b. Prove that the number of subsets of a set A with m elements is 2^m.

Question 7

a. Find $\sqrt{197}$. Give your answer correct to one decimal place

b. Hence determine whether 197 is prime.

Question 8

a. Find all prime numbers which divide 40!.

b. Find how many zeros are at the end of 40! when written as an integer.

Question 9

Prove that there are infinitely many prime numbers.

Question 10

Write $0.\dot{2}\dot{7}$ in the form $\frac{m}{n}$, where m and n are integers.

Question 11

Consider the set of numbers S of the form $n^2 - n + 41$ where $n \in Z^+$.

a. Prove that all elements of S are odd.

The first five elements of S are $\{41, 43, 47, 53, 61\}$. These are all prime numbers.

b. Show by use of a counterexample that not all elements of S are prime.

Question 12

Prove that $\log_2(3)$ is an irrational number.

Question 13

Prove that no positive integers m and n exist such that $m^2 - n^2 = 1$.

Question 14

a. By proving the contrapositive, prove that if n^2 is even then n is even.

b. By proving the contrapositive, prove that if $x^2 - 6x + 5$ is even then x is odd where $x \in Z$.

Question 15

Let $x, y \in R^+$. Prove that if $x \le y$, then $\sqrt{x} \le \sqrt{y}$.

Question 16

a. Let $x, y \in R$. Prove that if $x < y$, then $x < \frac{x+y}{2}$.

b. By using proof by contradiction and the part a. result, prove that $0.\dot{9} = 1$.

Question 17

Prove that for any prime $p \ge 5$, that $p^2 - 1$ is divisible by 12.

Question 18

Use mathematical induction to prove that $5 \times 7^n + 1$ is divisible by 6 $\forall n \in Z^+$.

Question 19

Use mathematical induction to prove that $\sum_{r=1}^{n}(r+1)2^{r-1} = n2^n$ $\forall n \in Z^+$.

Question 20

Use mathematical induction to prove that $2^n > n^3$ for $\forall n \in Z^+, n \ge 10$.

A2. Graph theory

Question 21

A simple, regular graph has 8 vertices.

Which of the following could **not** be the total number of edges?

A. 8 **B.** 16 **C.** 20 **D.** 24 **E.** 32

Question 22

Consider the graph with five isolated vertices shown below.

To form a tree, the minimum number of edges that must be added to the graph is

A. 1 **B.** 4 **C.** 5 **D.** 6 **E.** 10

[VCAA 2018 FM]

Question 23

A planar graph has five faces. This graph could have

A. eight vertices and eight edges

B. six vertices and eight edges

C. eight vertices and five edges

D. eight vertices and six edges

E. five vertices and eight edges

[VCAA 2018 FM]

Question 24

Consider the graph shown.

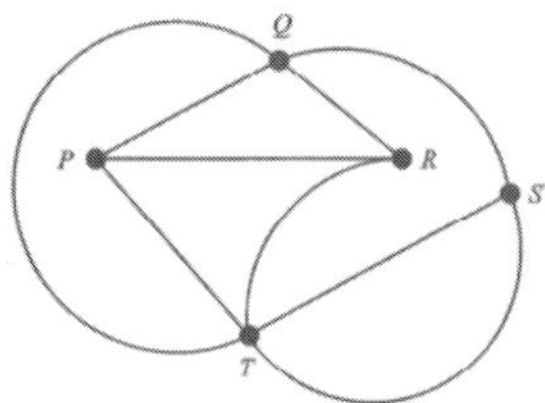

Which one of the following is **not** a path for this graph?

A. *PRQTS*

B. *PQRTS*

C. *PRTSQ*

D. *PTQSR*

E. *PTRQS*

[VCAA 2018 FM]

Question 25

Which one of the following graphs is **not** a planar graph?

A.

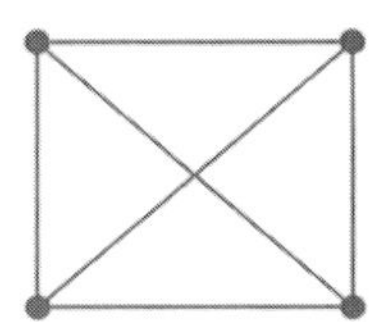

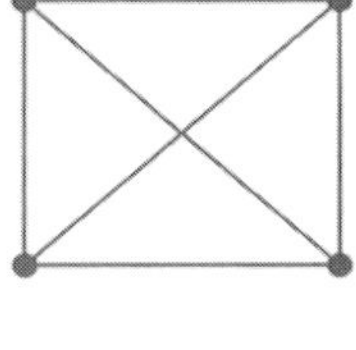

B.

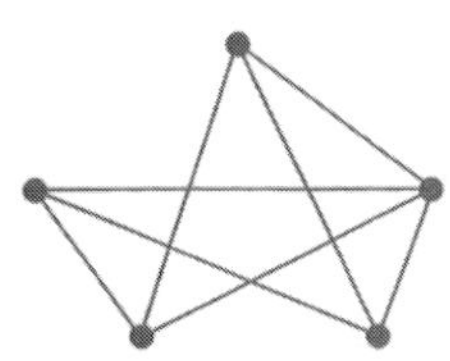

C.

D.

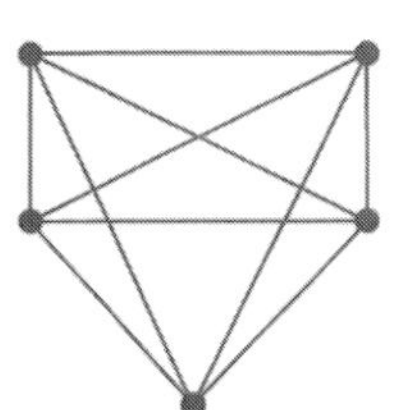

E.

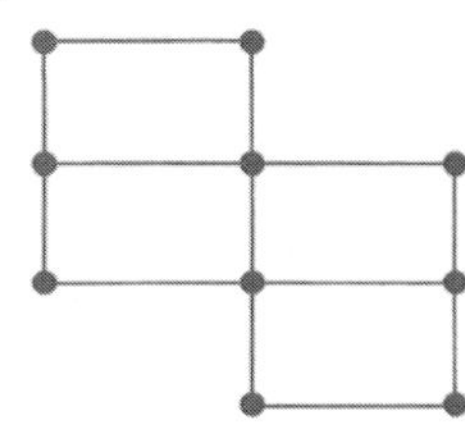

[VCAA 2018 FM]

Question 26

In the graph below, the sum of the degrees of the vertices is

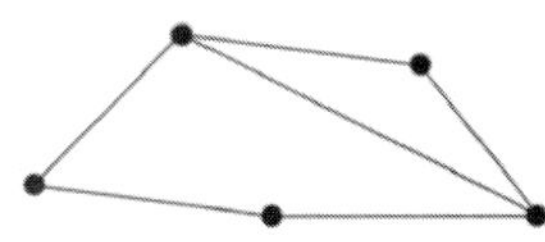

A. 5 **B.** 6 **C.** 10 **D.** 11 **E.** 12

[VCAA 2019 FM]

Question 27

Consider the graph below.

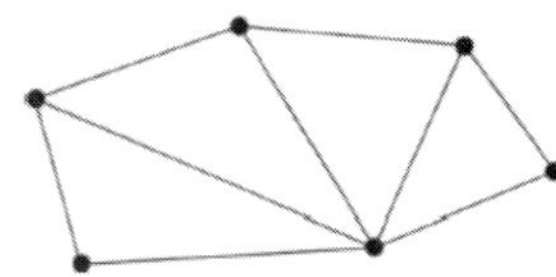

The minimum number of extra edges that are required so that an Eulerian circuit is possible in this graph is

A. 0 **B.** 1 **C.** 2 **D.** 3 **E.** 4

[VCAA 2019 FM]

A2. Graph theory

Question 28

Two graphs, labelled Graph 1 and Graph 2, are shown below.

Graph 1

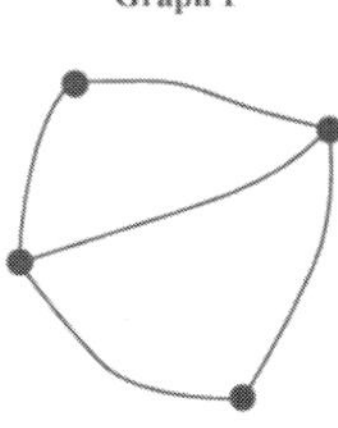

Graph 2

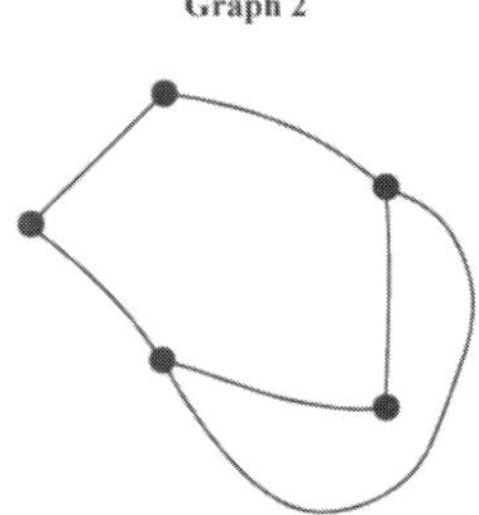

Which one of the following statements is **not** true?

A. Graph 1 and Graph 2 are isomorphic.

B. Graph 1 has five edges and Graph 2 has six edges.

C. Both Graph 1 and Graph 2 are connected graphs.

D. Both Graph 1 and Graph 2 have three faces each.

E. Neither Graph 1 nor Graph 2 are complete graphs.

[VCAA 2019 FM]

Question 29

The map below shows all the road connections between five towns, P, Q, R, S and T.

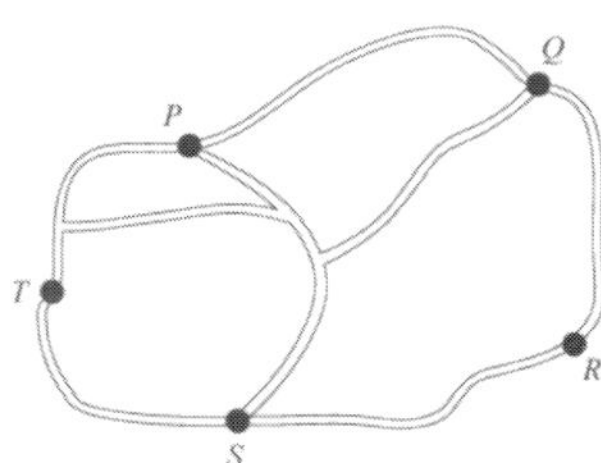

The road connections could be represented by the adjacency matrix

A.
$$\begin{array}{c} \\ P \\ Q \\ R \\ S \\ T \end{array}\begin{array}{c} \begin{array}{ccccc} P & Q & R & S & T \end{array} \\ \begin{bmatrix} 1 & 3 & 0 & 2 & 2 \\ 3 & 0 & 1 & 1 & 1 \\ 0 & 1 & 0 & 1 & 0 \\ 2 & 1 & 1 & 0 & 2 \\ 2 & 1 & 0 & 2 & 0 \end{bmatrix} \end{array}$$

B.
$$\begin{array}{c} \\ P \\ Q \\ R \\ S \\ T \end{array}\begin{array}{c} \begin{array}{ccccc} P & Q & R & S & T \end{array} \\ \begin{bmatrix} 1 & 2 & 0 & 2 & 2 \\ 2 & 0 & 1 & 1 & 1 \\ 0 & 1 & 0 & 1 & 0 \\ 2 & 1 & 1 & 0 & 2 \\ 2 & 1 & 0 & 2 & 0 \end{bmatrix} \end{array}$$

C.
$$\begin{array}{c} \\ P \\ Q \\ R \\ S \\ T \end{array}\begin{array}{c} \begin{array}{ccccc} P & Q & R & S & T \end{array} \\ \begin{bmatrix} 0 & 3 & 0 & 2 & 2 \\ 3 & 0 & 1 & 1 & 1 \\ 0 & 1 & 0 & 1 & 0 \\ 2 & 1 & 1 & 0 & 2 \\ 2 & 1 & 0 & 2 & 0 \end{bmatrix} \end{array}$$

D.
$$\begin{array}{c} \\ P \\ Q \\ R \\ S \\ T \end{array}\begin{array}{c} \begin{array}{ccccc} P & Q & R & S & T \end{array} \\ \begin{bmatrix} 0 & 2 & 0 & 2 & 2 \\ 2 & 0 & 1 & 1 & 1 \\ 0 & 1 & 0 & 1 & 0 \\ 2 & 1 & 1 & 0 & 2 \\ 2 & 1 & 0 & 2 & 0 \end{bmatrix} \end{array}$$

E.
$$\begin{array}{c} \\ P \\ Q \\ R \\ S \\ T \end{array}\begin{array}{c} \begin{array}{ccccc} P & Q & R & S & T \end{array} \\ \begin{bmatrix} 1 & 2 & 0 & 2 & 2 \\ 2 & 0 & 1 & 1 & 1 \\ 0 & 1 & 0 & 1 & 0 \\ 2 & 1 & 1 & 1 & 2 \\ 2 & 1 & 0 & 1 & 0 \end{bmatrix} \end{array}$$

[VCAA 2019 FM]

Question 30

A connected planar graph has seven vertices and nine edges.

The number of faces that this graph will have is

A. 1 **B.** 2 **C.** 3 **D.** 4 **E.** 5

[VCAA 2020 FM]

Question 31

Consider the graph below.

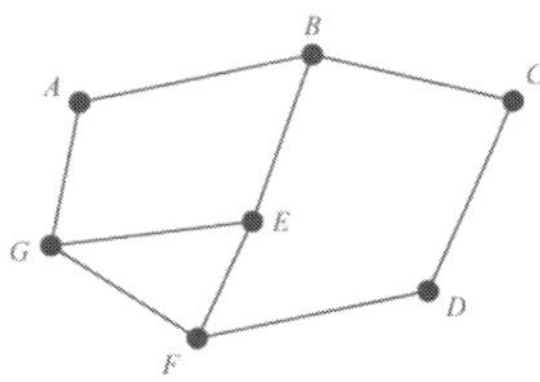

Which one of the following is **not** a Hamiltonian cycle for this graph?

A. *ABCDFEGA* **B.** *BAGEFDCB* **C.** *CDFEGABC* **D.** *DCBAGFED* **E.** *EGABCDFE*

[VCAA 2020 FM]

Question 32

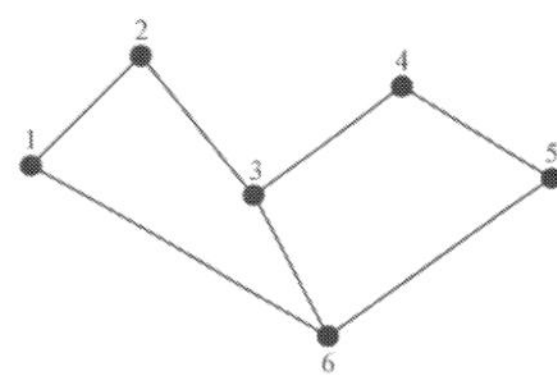

Which one of the following is **not** a spanning tree for the network above?

A.

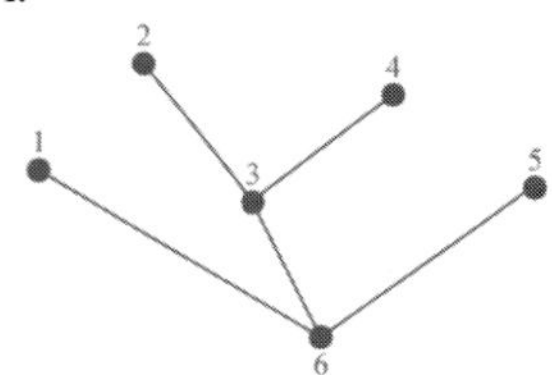

B.

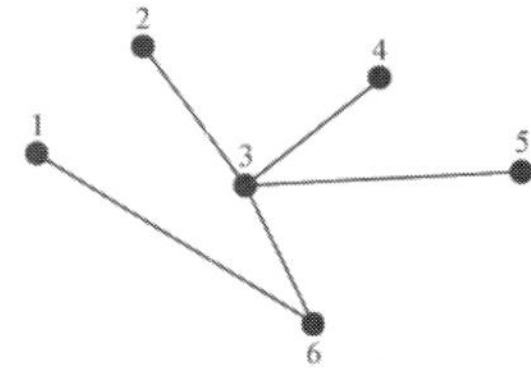

C.

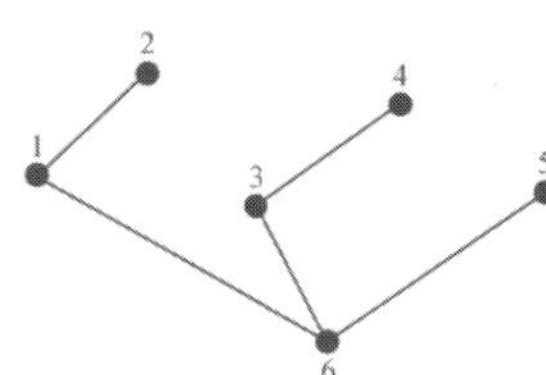

D.

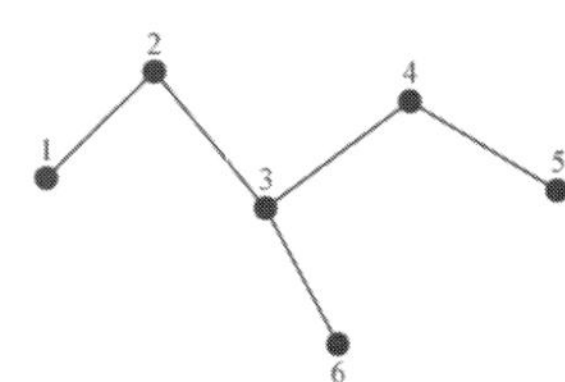

E.

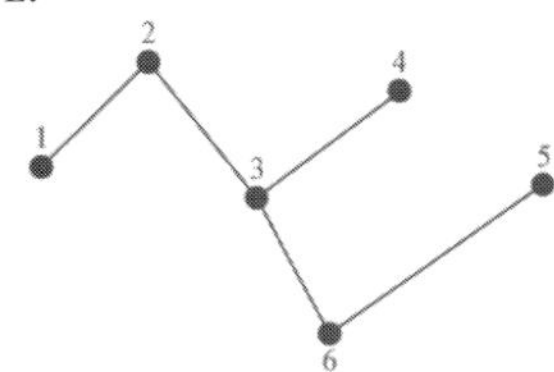

[VCAA 2020 FM]

Question 33

Four friends go to an ice-cream shop.

Akiro chooses chocolate and strawberry ice cream.

Doris chooses chocolate and vanilla ice cream.

Gohar chooses vanilla ice cream.

Imani chooses vanilla and lemon ice cream.

This information could be presented as a graph. Consider the following four statements:

- The graph would be connected.
- The graph would be bipartite.
- The graph would be planar.
- The graph would be a tree.

How many of these four statements are true?

A. 0 **B.** 1 **C.** 2 **D.** 3 **E.** 4

[VCAA 2020 FM]

Question 34

The adjacency matrix below shows the number of pathway connections between four landmarks: J, K, L and M.

$$\begin{array}{c} \\ J \\ K \\ L \\ M \end{array}\begin{array}{c} \begin{array}{cccc} J & K & L & M \end{array} \\ \begin{bmatrix} 1 & 3 & 0 & 2 \\ 3 & 0 & 1 & 2 \\ 0 & 1 & 0 & 2 \\ 2 & 2 & 2 & 0 \end{bmatrix} \end{array}$$

A network of pathways that could be represented by the adjacency matrix is

A.

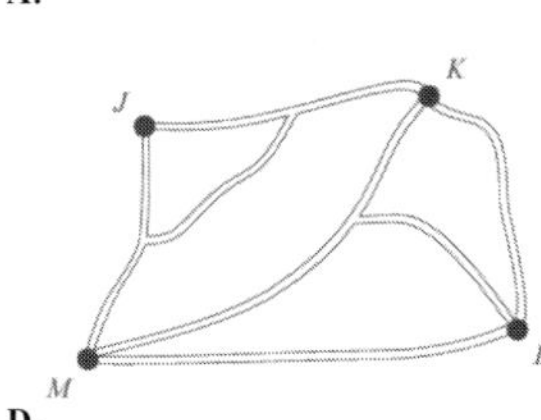

B.

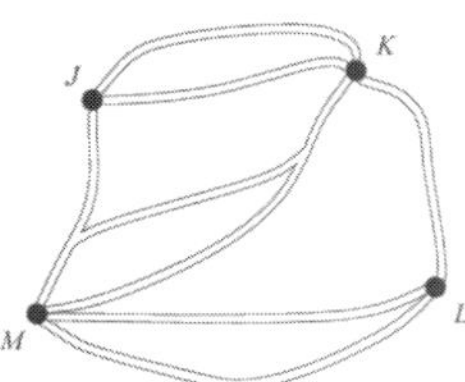

C.

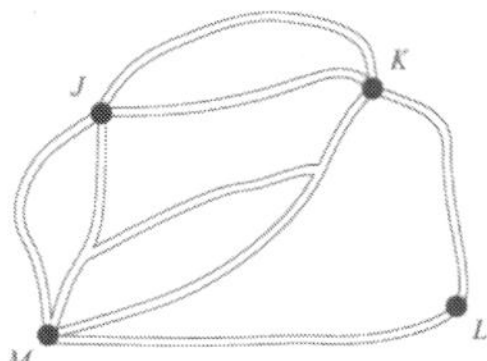

D.

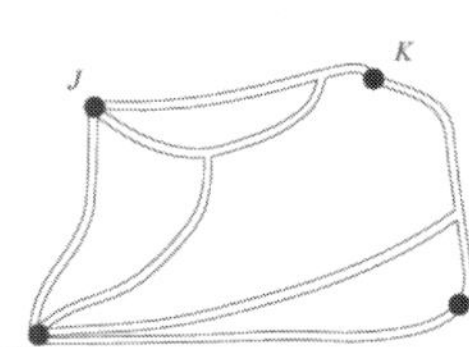

E.

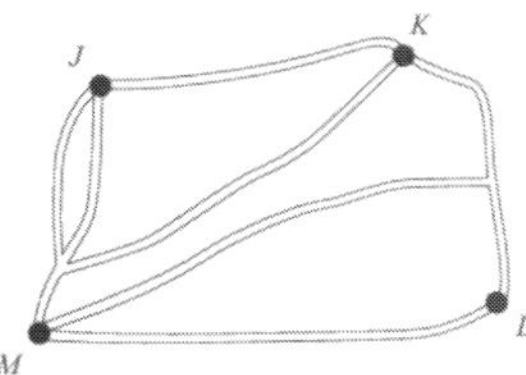

[VCAA 2020 FM]

Question 35

A tree T has 8 vertices.

a. State the number of edges T must have.

b. One of the vertices of T has degree 3 and another has degree 4. Determine how many different trees are possible in this case.

Question 36

Consider the graph G shown below.

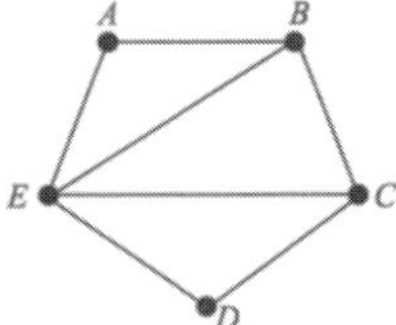

a. Explain why G has a Hamiltonian circuit but no Eulerian circuit.

A graph is **traversable** if it can be drawn without lifting pen from paper and without retracing any edge.

b. Explain why G is traversable and describe one way to draw it without lifting pen from paper.

Suppose that one edge is removed so that the resulting graph is traversable.

c. Explain which of G's edges **cannot** be removed.

d. Explain which edge of G **must** be removed if the resulting graph is to have an Eulerian circuit.

e. Suppose instead that one edge is added to G joining two of the existing vertices so that the resulting graph is simple and traversable. Explain where this edge could be placed.

f. Explain why G is planar and verify that it satisfies Euler's formula.

Question 37

Consider a simple connected graph G with v vertices.

a. Determine the minimum number of edges that G can have.

Consider K_n, the complete graph with n vertices.

b. State the number of edges in K_n.

c. State the number of edges in the complement of K_n.

Consider a graph H with n vertices and e edges.

d. Find an expression for the number of edges in H', the complement of H.

e. Hence show that a simple connected graph with n vertices and e edges satisfies the inequality $2n-2 \le 2e \le n^2-n$.

Question 38

By considering the number of edges in K_n and K_{n-1}, prove that any simple graph with n vertices and more than $\frac{1}{2}(n-1)(n-2)$ edges is connected.

Question 39

A simple graph is bipartite if and only if each circuit in the graph is of even length.

If G is a bipartite graph with an odd number of vertices, explain why G is not Hamiltonian.

Question 40

a. Prove by contradiction that $K_{3,3}$ is not planar.

Consider a simple connected graph G with $v \ge 3$ vertices.

b. Prove that if G is planar, then $e \le 3v-6$.

c. Hence deduce that K_5 is not planar.

Consider a simple connected graph H with at least 11 vertices.

d. Prove that H and its complement H' cannot both be planar.

A3. Logic and algorithms

Question 41

Which one of the following statements is **incorrect** if A, B and C are elements of a boolean algebra?

A. $A \cdot (B \cdot C) = (A \cdot B) \cdot C$

B. $A \cdot (B + C) = A \cdot B + A \cdot C$

C. $A \cdot A = A$

D. $(A + B)' = A' + B'$

E. $A \cdot (A + B) = A$

Question 42

The Venn diagram represents sets R, S and T.

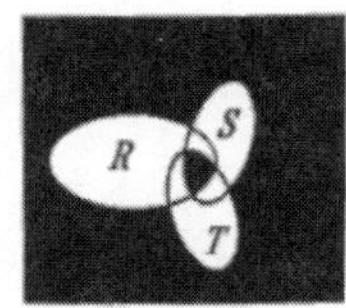

If the enclosing rectangle represents the universal set, then the shaded regions represent

A. $R \cap S \cap T$

B. $(R \cup S \cup T)'$

C. $(R \cap S \cap T) \cap (R' \cap S' \cap T')$

D. $(R \cap S \cap T) \cup (R' \cap S' \cap T')$

E. $(R \cap S \cap T) \cap (R' \cup S' \cup T')$

Question 43

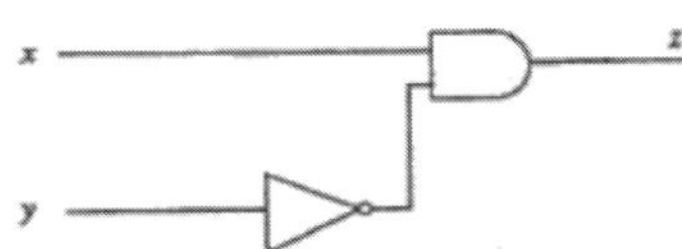

A table of inputs and outputs which corresponds to this circuit is

A.

x	y	z
0	0	0
1	0	0
0	1	1
1	1	0

B.

x	y	z
0	0	0
1	0	1
0	1	0
1	1	0

C.

x	y	z
0	0	1
1	0	0
0	1	0
1	1	1

D.

x	y	z
0	0	1
1	0	0
0	1	0
1	1	0

E.

x	y	z
0	0	1
1	0	1
0	1	1
1	1	0

A3. Logic and algorithms

Question 44

The boolean expression $\left(x' \cdot (y+z)\right)'$ is equivalent to

A. $x \cdot y + x \cdot z'$ **B.** $x + y' \cdot z'$ **C.** $x' + y \cdot z$ **D.** $x' \cdot y' + x' \cdot z'$ **E.** $x \cdot (y+z)'$

Question 45

For two propositions p and q, $\sim(p \vee q)$ is equivalent to

A. $\sim p \vee \sim q$ **B.** $\sim p \vee q$ **C.** $p \vee \sim q$ **D.** $p \wedge q$ **E.** $\sim p \wedge \sim q$

Question 46

For all values of X, Y and Z, the boolean expression $\left[(X \cup Y') \cap Z\right]'$ is equal to

A. $(X' \cap Y') \cap Z'$ **B.** $(X' \cap Y') \cup Z'$ **C.** $(X' \cap Y) \cap Z'$ **D.** $(X' \cup Y) \cap Z'$ **E.** $(X' \cap Y) \cup Z'$

Question 47

X	Y	Z
0	0	1
1	0	1
0	1	1
1	1	0

The expression that corresponds to the table of inputs and outputs above is

A. $(X \cup Y)'$ **B.** $(X \cap Y)'$ **C.** $X' \cup Y$ **D.** $X \cup Y'$ **E.** $X' \cap Y'$

Question 48

The boolean expression that corresponds to the Karnaugh map below is

		x	
		0	1
y	0	1	1
	1	1	1

A. $x' + x \cdot y$ **B.** $x + x' \cdot y$ **C.** $x' + x \cdot y'$ **D.** $x + x \cdot y$ **E.** $x' + x' \cdot y$

Question 49

The circuit that produces the same output as the one shown below is

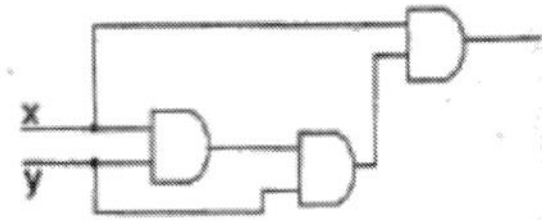

A.

B.

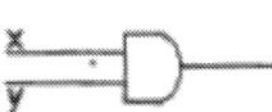

C.

D.

E.

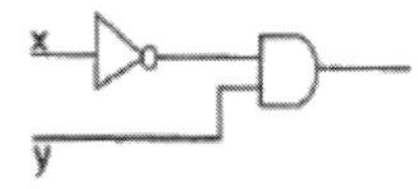

A3. Logic and algorithms

Question 50

If p is a proposition, then the proposition that is a tautology is

A. $\sim p \to p$ **B.** $\sim p \wedge p$ **C.** $\sim p \vee p$ **D.** $p \wedge p$ **E.** $p \vee p$

[VCAA 1994 SM]

Question 51

A switching circuit is expressed in simplest equivalent form when the equivalent circuit uses the least number of gates for any possible equivalent circuit.

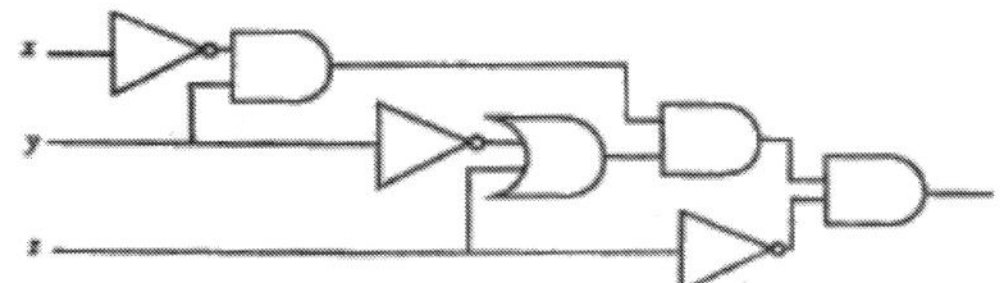

The boolean expression that represents the simplest equivalent form for the circuit shown above is

A. 0

B. $z' \cdot (z + y') + x' \cdot y$

C. 1

D. $x' \cdot y$

E. $x' + y'$

Question 52

The truth table for $y \to x$ is

A.

x	y	z
T	T	T
T	F	F
F	T	F
F	F	F

B.

x	y	z
T	T	T
T	F	F
F	T	F
F	F	T

C.

x	y	z
T	T	T
T	F	T
F	T	F
F	F	F

D.

x	y	z
0	0	1
1	0	0
0	1	0
1	1	0

E.

x	y	z
T	T	T
T	F	T
F	T	F
F	F	T

A3. Logic and algorithms

Question 53

Consider the following algorithm written in pseudocode.

```
x ← 1
while x < 50
    x ← 3x + 1
end while
print x
```

The output will be

A. 4 **B.** 5 **C.** 40 **D.** 121 **E.** 148

Question 54

Show that $y' + x' \cdot z + (x \cdot y)' = (x \cdot y)'$.

Question 55

a. On the Venn diagram, shade the region corresponding to $(X \cap Y' \cap Z) \cup (X' \cap Y' \cap Z)$.

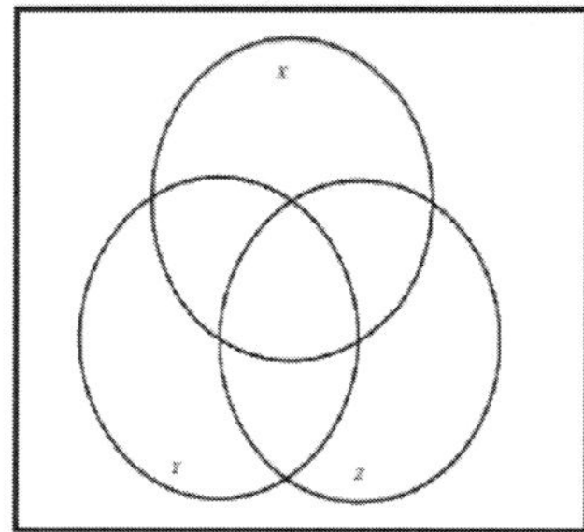

b. Hence or otherwise express $(X \cap Y' \cap Z) \cup (X' \cap Y' \cap Z)$ in simplest form.

Question 56

Draw a circuit that represents the boolean expression $(x + y) \cdot (x \cdot y)'$.

Question 57

a. Write in propositional logic notation an expression equivalent to the boolean expression $z = x \cdot y + (x' + y')$.

b. Complete the truth table corresponding to this propositional logic expression.

x	y	z
T	T	
T	F	
F	T	
F	F	

c. Is this expression a tautology? Explain.

d. Show that $x \cdot y + (x' + y') = 1$ using boolean algebraic techniques.

Question 58

Complete the truth table for $(A \vee B) \wedge \sim (A \wedge B)$.

A	B	$A \vee B$	$A \wedge B$	$\sim (A \wedge B)$	$(A \vee B) \wedge \sim (A \wedge B)$
T	T				
T	F				
F	T				
F	F				

Question 59

Let n be any natural number. Let p be the proposition that n is divisible by 4. Let q be the proposition that n is divisible by 100. Let s be the proposition that n is divisible by 400.

a. Complete the following table.

n	1900	1948	1995	2000
p	T			
q	T			
s	F			

In terms of n, what is meant by each of the following statements?

b. $\sim s$

c. $q \wedge \sim s$

d. $s \rightarrow p$

e. Complete the following table of truth values.

n	1900	1948	1995	2000
$\sim s$	T			
$q \wedge \sim s$	T			
$p \wedge \sim (q \wedge \sim s)$	F			
$s \rightarrow p$				T

f. Use the boolean algebra identity $(a \cdot b)' = a' + b'$ to show that $p \cdot (q \cdot s') = p \cdot q' + p \cdot s$.

[VCAA 1994 SM]

Question 60

a. Complete the Karnaugh map for $z = x' \cdot y' + x \cdot y' + x' \cdot y$.

		x	
		0	1
y	0		
	1		

b. Simplify the expression $z = x' \cdot y' + x \cdot y' + x' \cdot y$.

Question 61

Convert the decimal number 347 into binary form.

Question 62

Use the Euclidean algorithm to find the highest common factor of 56 and 315.

Question 63

Consider the polynomial $P(x) = 2x^3 - 7x^2 + 4x - 5$.

The following algorithm, known as Horner's method, can be applied to $P(x)$.

Step 1: Write $P(x)$ in order of decreasing powers of x.

Step 2: Factor x out of every non-constant term.

Step 3: Factor x out of every non-constant term in the innermost brackets.

Step 4: Repeat Step 3 until only a constant remains in the innermost brackets.

a. Use Horner's method to show that $((2x-7)x+4)x-5$.

b. Hence find $P(5)$.

c. By counting the number of operations required to evaluate $P(5)$, show that Horner's method is more efficient than direct evaluation.

Question 64

Write an algorithm that divides 470 by 9 and returns the quotient and remainder.

Question 65

Consider the sequence defined by the recurrence relation

$$t_{n+1} = 4t_n + 1, \ t_1 = 2.$$

a. Write an algorithm that will determine the smallest value of n for which $t_n > 2000$.

b. Perform a desk check to test your algorithm.

A4. Sequences and series

Question 66

Which one of the following sequences shows the first five terms of an arithmetic sequence?

A. $1, 2, 4, 8, 16, \ldots$

B. $1, 3, 7, 15, 31, \ldots$

C. $-4, -1, 1, 4, 7, \ldots$

D. $-7, -3, 1, 5, 9, \ldots$

E. $2, 3, 5, 8, 13, \ldots$

Question 67

In an arithmetic sequence, the second term is 46 and the fourth term is 32.

The first term is

A. 32 **B.** 39 **C.** 53 **D.** 60 **E.** 78

Question 68

The sum of the first 12 terms of the arithmetic sequence $-18, -8, 2, 12, \ldots$ is

A. -12 **B.** 92 **C.** 444 **D.** 504 **E.** 888

Question 69

Which one of the following is **not** a geometric sequence?

A. $1, 0.5, 0.25, 0.125, \ldots$

B. $1, 1.5, 1.25, 1.125, \ldots$

C. $-2, -2, -2, -2, \ldots$

D. $216, -72, 24, -8, \ldots$

E. $2, 2^3, 2^5, 2^7, \ldots$

Question 70

The first term of an infinite sequence is 60.

Each successive term is 25% of the value of the previous term.

The sum of the infinite sequence is

A. 60 **B.** 75 **C.** 80 **D.** 90 **E.** 240

Question 71

The number of flies in a laboratory is known to increase by 30% per day.

At 9 am on a Monday there were 200 flies in the laboratory.

At 9 am on the Wednesday of that week, the number of flies in the laboratory will be closest to

A. 230 **B.** 260 **C.** 320 **D.** 338 **E.** 439

Question 72

Ten pieces of wood are needed to make the 'steps' of an old-fashioned ladder. The first step is 50 cm in length. The next step is 2 cm shorter (1 cm at each end). This pattern is followed for all 10 steps. The total length of wood required, in cm, is equal to

A. 410 **B.** 600 **C.** 680 **D.** 710 **E.** 850

A4. Sequences and series

Question 73

A sequence follows the rule $w_{n+1} = 4w_n$, where w_n is the nth term and $n = 1, 2, 3, 4, \ldots$.

If $w_2 = 12$, then w_4 is equal to

A. 3 **B.** 12 **C.** 48 **D.** 192 **E.** 200

Question 74

The following recurrence relation can generate a sequence of numbers.

$$L_0 = 37, \qquad L_{n+1} = L_n + C$$

The value of L_2 is 25.

The value of C is

A. –6 **B.** –4 **C.** 4 **D.** 6 **E.** 37

[VCAA 2021 FM]

Question 75

A geometric sequence has first term a and common ratio r where $r \neq 1$.

The first, second and fourth terms of the geometric sequence form the first three terms of an arithmetic sequence with common difference d.

a. Show that $r^3 - 2r + 1 = 0$.

b. Find the values of b and c such that $r^3 - 2r + 1 = (r-1)(r^2 + br + c)$.

c. Given that the sum of the geometric sequence is convergent, find the exact value of r.

d. Given also that $S_\infty = 3 + \sqrt{5}$, find the value of a.

Question 76

The first term of a geometric sequence is 10 and the common ratio is 0.8.

a. Find the fifth term.

b. Find the sum of the first 25 terms, giving your answer correct to one decimal place.

Let S_n denote the sum of the first n terms and let S_∞ denote the sum to infinity.

c. Find the least value of n such that $S_\infty - S_n < 0.01$.

Question 77

The sequence $4, 5, 7, \ldots$ is generated by a recurrence relation of the form

$$t_{n+1} = at_n + b, \; t_1 = 4.$$

a. Find the values of a and b.

b. Hence find the fourth term of the sequence.

The nth term of the sequence is given by the general formula $t_n = a^{n-1}t_1 + \dfrac{b(a^{n-1} - 1)}{a-1}$.

c. Use this general formula to verify your answer to part (b).

Question 78

Consider the sequence defined by the recurrence relation

$$t_{n+1} = 3t_n + 1, \ t_1 = 2.$$

a. Find a formula for the nth term of the sequence.
Give your answer in the form $t_n = Ar^{n-1} + B$ where A, B are constants to be determined.

b. Hence determine the first four terms of the sequence.

c. Describe what happens to t_n for large values of n.

Question 79

Thuong borrows \$60 000 at an interest rate of 8.5% per annum, adjusted monthly, with monthly repayments of \$550.

The recurrence relation that describes the amount, $\$A_n$, owed by Thuong at the start of the nth month is of the form

$$A_{n+1} = rA_n - d, \ A_1 = a.$$

a. Write down the values of a and d.

b. Find the value of r.

c. Write down an expression for A_n in terms of n.

d. Determine the number of repayments required for Thuong to pay off the loan.

Question 80

At the start of a year, a dam is estimated to contain 600 carp. The owner of the dam estimates that the number of carp will increase on average by 10% per year. At the end of each year, the owner decides to remove 50 carp from the dam.

The recurrence relation that models the number of carp, C_n, in the dam at the start of the nth year is of the form

$$C_{n+1} = rC_n - d, \ C_1 = 600.$$

a. Write down the values of r and d.

b. Use this model to predict the number of carp in the dam after five years.

c. Determine when the number of carp in the dam will first exceed 1000.

Suppose that the dam owner decides instead to remove 75 carp from the dam at the end of each year.

d. Write down a new recurrence relation that models the number of carp in the dam.

e. Determine when the carp will disappear from the dam.

f. Determine what would happen to the carp population if the dam owner removed 60 carp at the end of each year.

A5. Combinatorics

Question 81

The expression $\frac{^nP_r}{^nP_{r-1}}$ is equal to

A. $\frac{n-r+1}{r}$ **B.** $\frac{1}{n-r}$ **C.** $\frac{1}{r}$

D. $n-r+1$ **E.** $\frac{1}{n-r+1}$

Question 82

Four letters are randomly chosen from the word RESOLUTE.

The probability that exactly three of these letters will be vowels is

A. $\frac{3}{8}$ **B.** $\frac{2}{35}$ **C.** $\frac{4}{35}$ **D.** $\frac{8}{35}$ **E.** $\frac{3}{70}$

Question 83

Each of the 18 students in a Year 11 class studies Biology, Chemistry or Physics. Of these students, 7 study Biology, 10 study Chemistry and 10 study Physics. Also, 3 study Biology and Chemistry, 4 study Biology and Physics and 5 study Chemistry and Physics.

If one student studies all three subjects, then the number of students who study none of these subjects is equal to

A. 1 **B.** 2 **C.** 4 **D.** 14 **E.** 16

Question 84

A group of three students is selected randomly from a group of four boys and five girls.

The number of groups that would have more girls than boys is equal to

A. 10 **B.** 40 **C.** 50 **D.** 84 **E.** 400

Question 85

Allowing the empty set to be a subset, the number of subsets containing at least two elements that can be formed from the set S where $S = \{1, 2, 3, ..., 8, 9, 10\}$ is equal to

A. 10 **B.** $10!-11$ **C.** 2^{10}

D. $2^{10}-10$ **E.** $2^{10}-11$

Question 86

Some friends chose some take away curries. They like the look of three different lamb curries and four different chicken curries.

If they chose four different curries in total and at least one is lamb and at least two are chicken, then the number of different possible selections is

A. 16 **B.** 30 **C.** 35 **D.** 48 **E.** 144

Question 87

Peter asks his friend John to choose 27 distinct positive odd integers all less than 100.

Peter claims that John will have a pair of numbers whose sum is equal to 102.

Use the pigeonhole principle to show that Peter's claim is correct.

Question 88

In how many ways can 4 girls and 3 boys be arranged in a row of seats if

a. they are placed randomly?

b. the 4 girls are seated together and the 3 boys are seated together?

c. no girl is seated next to another girl?

Question 89

Show that in a group of 15 people, at least three were born on the same day of the week.

Question 90

Show that ${}^{n}C_{r} + {}^{n}C_{r-1} = {}^{n+1}C_{r}$ where $1 \le r \le n$.

Question 91

In a group of 110 students, 30 study Accounting, 35 study Biology and 20 study both.

a. Find the number of students that study either Accounting or Biology.

b. Hence find the number of students who do not study either subject.

Question 92

A bag contains nine cards numbered 1, 2, 3, 4, 5, 6, 7, 8, 9.

Grant chooses four cards at random, without replacement, and places them in a row.

a. How many different four-digit numbers can be formed?

b. How many different odd four-digit numbers can be formed?

Grant's four cards are put back in the bag. Julie then chooses four cards at random, without replacement.

c. Find the probability that the four cards display at least three odd digits.

d. Find the probability that the digits on the four cards add up to 28.

Question 93

How many six-letter words can be formed by using the letters of the word GUESSES?

Question 94

Use the inclusion-exclusion principle to find the number of integers from 1 to 200 inclusive that are not divisible by 2, 3 or 5.

Question 95

Show that ${}^{n+1}P_{r} = {}^{n}P_{r} + r \times {}^{n}P_{r-1}$.

A6. Matrices

Question 96

Which one of the following matrices has a determinant of zero?

A. $\begin{bmatrix} 0 & 1 \\ 1 & 0 \end{bmatrix}$ **B.** $\begin{bmatrix} 1 & 0 \\ 0 & 1 \end{bmatrix}$ **C.** $\begin{bmatrix} 1 & 2 \\ -3 & 6 \end{bmatrix}$

D. $\begin{bmatrix} 3 & 6 \\ 2 & 4 \end{bmatrix}$ **E.** $\begin{bmatrix} 4 & 0 \\ 0 & -2 \end{bmatrix}$

[VCAA 2018 FM]

Question 97

Liam cycles, runs, swims and walks for exercise several times a month.

Each time he cycles, Liam covers a distance of c kilometres.

Each time he runs, Liam covers a distance of r kilometres.

Each time he swims, Liam covers a distance of s kilometres.

Each time he walks, Liam covers a distance of w kilometres.

The number of times that Liam cycled, ran, swam and walked each month over a four-month period, and the total distance that Liam travelled in each of these months, are shown in the table below.

	Number of times in a month				
	Cycle	**Run**	**Swim**	**Walk**	**Total distance for a month (km)**
Month 1	5	7	6	8	160
Month 2	8	6	9	7	172
Month 3	7	8	7	6	165
Month 4	8	8	5	5	162

The matrix that contains the distance each time Liam cycled, ran, swam and walked, $\begin{bmatrix} c \\ r \\ s \\ w \end{bmatrix}$, is

A. $\begin{bmatrix} 5 \\ 6 \\ 7 \\ 5 \end{bmatrix}$ **B.** $\begin{bmatrix} 8 \\ 6 \\ 1 \\ 9 \end{bmatrix}$ **C.** $\begin{bmatrix} 8 \\ 6 \\ 7 \\ 9 \end{bmatrix}$

D. $\begin{bmatrix} 8 \\ 8 \\ 9 \\ 8 \end{bmatrix}$ **E.** $\begin{bmatrix} 4290 \\ 4931 \\ 4623 \\ 4291 \end{bmatrix}$

[VCAA 2018 FM]

Question 98

Consider the following four matrix expressions.

$$\begin{bmatrix}8\\12\end{bmatrix}+\begin{bmatrix}4\\2\end{bmatrix} \qquad \begin{bmatrix}8\\12\end{bmatrix}+\begin{bmatrix}4&0\\0&2\end{bmatrix}$$

$$\begin{bmatrix}8&0\\12&0\end{bmatrix}+\begin{bmatrix}4\\2\end{bmatrix} \qquad \begin{bmatrix}8&0\\12&0\end{bmatrix}+\begin{bmatrix}4&0\\0&2\end{bmatrix}$$

How many of these four matrix expressions are defined?

A. 0 **B.** 1 **C.** 2 **D.** 3 **E.** 4

[VCAA 2019 FM]

Question 99

There are two rides called The Big Dipper and The Terror Train at a carnival.

The cost, in dollars, for a child to ride on each ride is shown in the table below.

Ride	Cost ($)
The Big Dipper	7
The Terror Train	8

Six children ride once only on The Big Dipper and once only on The Terror Train.

The total cost of the rides, in dollars, for these six children can be determined by which one of the following calculations?

A. $[6]\times[7\ \ 8]$

B. $[6]\times\begin{bmatrix}7\\8\end{bmatrix}$

C. $[6\ \ 6]\times[7\ \ 8]$

D. $[6\ \ 6]\times\begin{bmatrix}7\\8\end{bmatrix}$

E. $\begin{bmatrix}6\\6\end{bmatrix}\times[7\ \ 8]$

[VCAA 2019 FM]

Question 100

Consider the matrix P, where $P=\begin{bmatrix}3&2&1\\5&4&3\end{bmatrix}$.

The element in row i and column j of matrix P is p_{ij}.

The elements in matrix P are determined by the rule

A. $p_{ij}=4-j$

B. $p_{ij}=2i+1$

C. $p_{ij}=i+j+1$

D. $p_{ij}=i+2j$

E. $p_{ij}=2i-j+2$

[VCAA 2019 FM]

Question 101

$$\begin{bmatrix} 2 & 2 & 0 & -2 \\ 2 & 0 & -2 & 0 \\ 0 & 2 & 0 & -2 \\ 2 & 2 & -2 & 0 \end{bmatrix} \begin{bmatrix} v \\ w \\ x \\ y \end{bmatrix} = \begin{bmatrix} 2 \\ 6 \\ -8 \\ 4 \end{bmatrix}$$

Which one of the following systems of simultaneous linear equations best represents the matrix equation above?

A. $\begin{aligned} 2v+2w-2y &= 2 \\ 2v-2x &= 6 \\ 2v-2y &= -8 \\ 2v+2w-2x &= 4 \end{aligned}$

B. $\begin{aligned} 2v+2w-2y &= 2 \\ 2v-2x &= 6 \\ 2w-2y &= -8 \\ 2v+2w-2x &= 4 \end{aligned}$

C. $\begin{aligned} 2v+2w+2y &= 2 \\ 2v-2x &= 6 \\ 2w-2y &= -8 \\ 2v+2w-2x &= 4 \end{aligned}$

D. $\begin{aligned} 2v+2w-2y &= 2 \\ 2v-2x &= 6 \\ 2w-2y &= -8 \\ 2v+2w+2x &= 4 \end{aligned}$

E. $\begin{aligned} 2v+2w-2y &= 2 \\ 2v-2w &= 6 \\ 2w-2y &= -8 \\ 2v+2w-2x &= 4 \end{aligned}$

[VCAA 2019 FM]

Question 102

Matrix $A = \begin{bmatrix} 1 & 2 \\ 0 & 3 \\ 1 & 0 \\ 4 & 5 \end{bmatrix}$ and matrix $B = \begin{bmatrix} 2 & 0 & 3 & 1 \\ 4 & 5 & 2 & 0 \end{bmatrix}$.

Matrix $Q = A \times B$.

The element in row i and column j of matrix Q is q_{ij}.

Element q_{41} is determined by the calculation

A. $0\times0+3\times5$ **B.** $1\times1+2\times0$ **C.** $1\times2+2\times4$ **D.** $4\times1+5\times0$ **E.** $4\times2+5\times4$

[VCAA 2020 FM]

Question 103

Matrices P and W are defined below.

$$P = \begin{bmatrix} 0 & 0 & 1 & 0 & 0 \\ 0 & 0 & 0 & 0 & 1 \\ 0 & 1 & 0 & 0 & 0 \\ 0 & 0 & 0 & 1 & 0 \\ 1 & 0 & 0 & 0 & 0 \end{bmatrix} \qquad W = \begin{bmatrix} A \\ S \\ T \\ O \\ R \end{bmatrix}$$

If $P^n \times W = \begin{bmatrix} A \\ S \\ T \\ O \\ R \end{bmatrix}$, the value of n could be

A. 1 **B.** 2 **C.** 3 **D.** 4 **E.** 5

[VCAA 2020 FM]

Question 104

The element in row i and column j of matrix M is m_{ij}.

M is a 3×3 matrix. It is constructed using the rule $m_{ij} = 3i + 2j$.

M is

A. $\begin{bmatrix} 5 & 7 & 9 \\ 7 & 9 & 11 \\ 11 & 13 & 15 \end{bmatrix}$ **B.** $\begin{bmatrix} 5 & 7 & 9 \\ 8 & 10 & 12 \\ 11 & 13 & 15 \end{bmatrix}$ **C.** $\begin{bmatrix} 5 & 7 & 10 \\ 8 & 10 & 13 \\ 11 & 13 & 16 \end{bmatrix}$

D. $\begin{bmatrix} 5 & 8 & 11 \\ 7 & 10 & 13 \\ 9 & 12 & 15 \end{bmatrix}$ **E.** $\begin{bmatrix} 5 & 8 & 11 \\ 8 & 11 & 14 \\ 11 & 14 & 17 \end{bmatrix}$

[VCAA 2020 FM]

Question 105

$$ax + 4y = 10$$
$$18x + by = 6$$

The set of simultaneous linear equations above does not have a unique solution when

A. $a = 2, b = 36$

B. $a = 3, b = 22$

C. $a = 4, b = 20$

D. $a = 5, b = 12$

E. $a = 6, b = 14$

[VCAA 2021 FM]

Question 106

The car park at a theme park has three areas, A, B and C.

The number of empty (E) and full (F) parking spaces in each of the three areas at 1 pm on Friday are shown in matrix Q below.

$$\begin{array}{cc} & \begin{array}{cc} E & F \end{array} \\ Q = & \begin{bmatrix} 70 & 50 \\ 30 & 20 \\ 40 & 40 \end{bmatrix} \begin{array}{l} A \\ B \\ C \end{array} \textit{ area} \end{array}$$

a. What is the order of matrix Q?

b. Write down a calculation to show that 110 parking spaces are full at 1 pm.

Drivers must pay a parking fee for each hour of parking.

Matrix P, below, shows the hourly fee, in dollars, for a car parked in each of the three areas.

$$\begin{array}{cc} & \textit{area} \\ & \begin{array}{ccc} A & B & C \end{array} \\ P = & \begin{bmatrix} 1.30 & 3.50 & 1.80 \end{bmatrix} \end{array}$$

c. The total parking fee, in dollars, collected from these 110 parked cars if they were parked for one hour is calculated as follows.

$$P \times L = \begin{bmatrix} 207.00 \end{bmatrix}$$

where matrix L is a 3×1 matrix.

Write down matrix L.

[VCAA 2019 FM]

Question 107

The matrix A is given by $A=\begin{bmatrix} k & 3 \\ -2 & 1 \end{bmatrix}$.

a. Given that A is singular, find the value of k.

b. Given instead that A is non-singular, find A^{-1} and hence solve the system of linear equations

$$\begin{aligned} kx+3y&=1 \\ -2x+y&=-1 \end{aligned}.$$

Question 108

Given that A and B are non-singular square matrices and I is the identity matrix, show that

a. $AB\left(A^{-1}B\right)^{-1}=A^2$.

b. $B\left(AB\right)^{-1}A-I=O$ where O is the zero matrix.

Question 109

The matrix A is given by $A=\begin{bmatrix} 2 & 1 & 1 \\ 0 & 3 & 4 \\ 6 & 0 & 1 \end{bmatrix}$ and the matrix B is given $B=\begin{bmatrix} 3 & -1 & 1 \\ 24 & -4 & -8 \\ -18 & 6 & 6 \end{bmatrix}$.

a. Find AB.

b. Hence solve the system of linear equations

$$\begin{aligned} 2x+y+z&=-1 \\ 3y+4z&=-7 \\ 6x+z&=8 \end{aligned}.$$

Question 110

The matrix A is given by $A=\begin{bmatrix} 2 & 1 \\ 7 & 4 \end{bmatrix}$.

a. Find the values of p and q such that $pI+qA+A^2=O$ where $I=\begin{bmatrix} 1 & 0 \\ 0 & 1 \end{bmatrix}$ and $O=\begin{bmatrix} 0 & 0 \\ 0 & 0 \end{bmatrix}$.

b. Use the result from part a. to show that A is non-singular and hence find A^{-1}.

c. Find a matrix X such that $AX=\begin{bmatrix} 1 & 1 \\ -1 & 0 \end{bmatrix}$.

B1. Simulation, sampling and sampling distributions

Question 111

Phil buys boxes of breakfast cereal; each box contains the picture of one football star.

There are 12 football stars in all, and their pictures are randomly distributed among the boxes of cereal.

Phil is only interested in one picture, so he assumes that there is a $\frac{1}{12}$ chance of finding this picture in a box of cereal that he buys.

He wants to estimate how many boxes he expects to have to buy to get this picture.

Which of the following simulation procedures could Phil use?

A. Roll two dice until he gets a sum of 12.

B. Roll two dice until he gets a sum of 11.

C. Roll two dice until he gets a sum of 11 or more.

D. Roll two dice until he gets a product of 12.

E. Roll two dice until he gets the same number on each of the dice.

Question 112

A polling company wants to estimate the proportion of voters in a particular electorate of 20 000 enrolled voters who intend voting for the party of government. They intend to sample 100 voters.

Which of the following could constitute a simple random sample?

A. Randomly select 100 individuals as they exit the local train station at peak hour.

B. Text 100 individuals selected at random from a telemarketing list.

C. Using the electoral roll, select every 200th individual starting at a random point.

D. Using the electoral roll, randomly select 50 males and 50 females from the roll.

E. Using the electoral roll, randomly select 100 individuals from the roll.

Question 113

The random variable X has the following probability distribution, where $0 < p < \frac{1}{3}$.

x	-1	0	1
$\Pr(X = x)$	p	$2p$	$1-3p$

The variance of X is

A. $2p(1-3p)$

B. $1-4p$

C. $(1-3p)^2$

D. $6p-16p^2$

E. $p(5-9p)$

[VCAA 2017 MM]

B1. Simulation, sampling and sampling distributions

Question 114

The discrete random variable X has the following probability distribution.

x	0	1	2	3
$\Pr(X=x)$	a	$3a$	$5a$	$7a$

The mean of X is

A. $\frac{1}{16}$ **B.** 1 **C.** $\frac{35}{16}$ **D.** $\frac{17}{8}$ **E.** 2

[VCAA 2019 MM]

Question 115

Let X be a random variable with mean μ and variance σ^2.

X_1, X_2, X_3 are independent random variables with identical distributions to X.

Which one of the following statements is correct?

A. $\mathrm{E}(X_1+X_2+X_3)=3\mu$ and $\mathrm{Var}(X_1+X_2+X_3)=3\sigma^2$

B. $\mathrm{E}(X_1+X_2+X_3)=3\mu$ and $\mathrm{Var}(X_1+X_2+X_3)=\sqrt{3}\sigma^2$

C. $\mathrm{E}(X_1+X_2+X_3)=3\mu$ and $\mathrm{Var}(X_1+X_2+X_3)=\sqrt{3}\sigma$

D. $\mathrm{E}(X_1+X_2+X_3)=\mu$ and $\mathrm{Var}(X_1+X_2+X_3)=3\sigma^2$

E. $\mathrm{E}(X_1+X_2+X_3)=\mu$ and $\mathrm{Var}(X_1+X_2+X_3)=\sqrt{3}\sigma$

Question 116

Let X be a random variable with mean μ and variance σ^2.

X_1, X_2 are independent random variables with identical distributions to X.

Which one of the following statements is incorrect?

A. $\mathrm{E}(X_1+X_2)=2\mathrm{E}(X)$

B. $\mathrm{Var}(X_1+X_2)=4\mathrm{Var}(X)$

C. $\mathrm{Var}(X_1+X_2)=2\mathrm{Var}(X)$

D. $\mathrm{Var}(2X)=4\mathrm{Var}(X)$

E. $\mathrm{E}(X_1+X_2)=\mathrm{E}(2X)$

Question 117

Which of the following is a **true** statement?

A. Population statistics are used to estimate population parameters.

B. Population parameters are used to estimate population statistics.

C. Sample statistics are used to estimate population parameters.

D. Sample parameters are used to estimate population statistics.

E. Sample statistics are used to estimate sample parameters.

B1. Simulation, sampling and sampling distributions

Question 118

Let X be a random variable with mean $\mu = 27$ and standard deviation $\sigma = 9$.

The mean and standard deviation of the sample mean $\bar{X}$ for random samples of size $n = 36$ are

A. $\text{E}(\bar{X}) = 27$, $\text{sd}(\bar{X}) = 9$

B. $\text{E}(\bar{X}) = 0.75$, $\text{sd}(\bar{X}) = 0.25$

C. $\text{E}(\bar{X}) = 27$, $\text{sd}(\bar{X}) = 1.5$

D. $\text{E}(\bar{X}) = 27$, $\text{sd}(\bar{X}) = 0.25$

E. $\text{E}(\bar{X}) = 4.5$, $\text{sd}(\bar{X}) = 1.5$

Question 119

Which one of the following statements is correct about a population mean μ and a sample mean $\bar{x}$ associated with repeated random samples of the same size from the same population?

A. The population mean μ will vary from sample to sample.

B. The sample mean $\bar{x}$ will not vary from sample to sample.

C. The population mean μ and the sample mean $\bar{x}$ may vary from sample to sample.

D. The sample mean $\bar{x}$ will vary from sample to sample.

E. The population mean μ and the sample mean $\bar{x}$ do not vary from sample to sample.

Question 120

Health researchers were interested in the amount of sugar consumed by people in their city.

They suspected it may be more than the 20 teaspoons per day average of the general population.

They randomly selected 100 people from their city and found their average daily sugar consumption was 24 teaspoons per day.

a. What is the value of the population mean μ?

b. What is the value of the sample mean $\bar{x}$?

Question 121

The probability distribution of a discrete random variable, X, is given by the table below.

x	0	1	2	3	4
$\Pr(X = x)$	0.2	$0.6p^2$	0.1	$1-p$	0.1

a. Show that $p = \frac{2}{3}$ or $p = 1$.

b. Let $p = \frac{2}{3}$.

i. Calculate $\text{E}(X)$.

ii. Find $\Pr(X \geq \text{E}(X))$.

[VCAA 2013 MM (CAS)]

Question 122

Let X be a random variable with mean $\mu = 6$ and variance $\sigma^2 = 4$.

If X_1, X_2, X_3 are independent random variables with identical distributions to X, find the mean and standard deviation of $X_1 + 2X_2 + X_3$.

B1. Simulation, sampling and sampling distributions

Question 123

The following table gives the probability distribution of X, the number observed when a tetrahedral die is rolled.

x	1	2	3	4
$\Pr(X = x)$	$\frac{1}{4}$	$\frac{1}{4}$	$\frac{1}{4}$	$\frac{1}{4}$

Suppose that this die is rolled twice.

a. Find the mean and variance of X, the number observed from one roll.

b. Find the probability distribution of $X_1 + X_2$, the sum of the two numbers obtained from two rolls of the die.

c. Find the probability that the sum of the two numbers obtained is odd.

d. Find the mean and variance of $X_1 + X_2$.

Question 124

Let X be a random variable with mean μ and variance σ^2.

Consider the sample mean $\bar{X}$ for random samples of size n.

a. Prove that $\mathrm{E}(\bar{X}) = \mu$.

b. Prove that $\mathrm{Var}(\bar{X}) = \dfrac{\sigma^2}{n}$.

Question 125

In a large city, the number of students in high school mathematics classes has mean $\mu = 20$ and standard deviation $\sigma = 4$.

The following dotplot shows the sample means, $\bar{x}$, for 50 random samples of 25 classes.

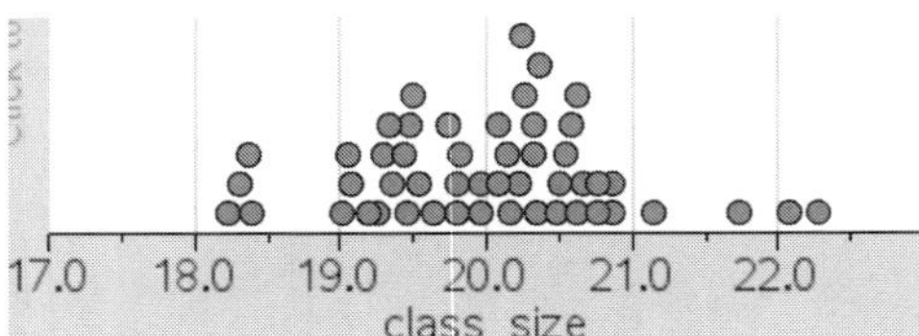

Use the dotplot to estimate:

a. $\Pr(\bar{X} \geq 21)$.

b. $\Pr(18.5 \leq \bar{X} \leq 21)$.

B2. Trigonometry

Question 126

The pie chart below displays the results of a survey.

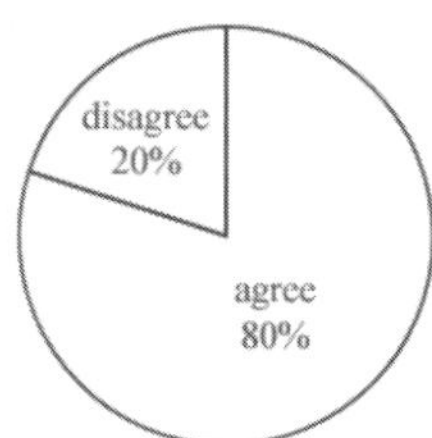

Eighty per cent of the people surveyed selected 'agree'.

Twenty per cent of the people surveyed selected 'disagree'.

The radius of the pie chart is 16 mm.

The area of the sector representing 'agree', in square millimetres, is closest to

A. 80 **B.** 161 **C.** 483 **D.** 643 **E.** 804

[VCAA 2020 FM]

Question 127

An 80 m high lookout tower stands in the centre of town.

Two landmarks, on the same horizontal plane, are visible from the top of the lookout tower.

The direct distance from the top of the lookout tower to the base of Landmark A is 170 m.

The direct distance from the top of the lookout tower to the base of Landmark B is 234 m.

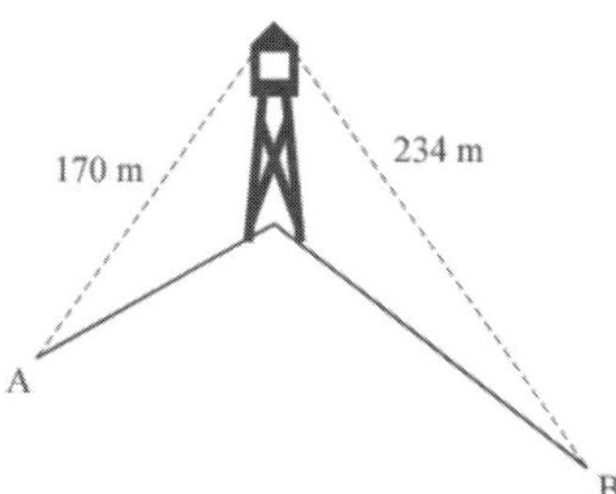

The bearing of Landmark B from Landmark A is 105°.

The bearing of Landmark B from the lookout tower is 142°.

The direct distance along the ground, in metres, between Landmark A and landmark B is closest to

A. 127 **B.** 135 **C.** 246 **D.** 297 **E.** 320

[VCAA 2020 FM]

Question 128

Rod and Lucia went on a bushwalk.

They walked 1400 m from the car park to reach a lookout that was directly east of the car park.

From the lookout, Rod returned to the car park via a cafe and Lucia returned to the car park via a swimming hole.

- The bearing of the swimming hole from the lookout is 290°.
- The bearing of the cafe from the lookout is 240°.
- The swimming hole is 950 m from the car park.
- The cafe is 700 m from the car park.
- The swimming hole is closer to the lookout than it is to the car park.

In relation to the total distance each of them individually walked from the lookout back to the car park, which one of the following statements is true?

A. Rod and Lucia walked the same distance.

B. Rod walked 467 m further than Lucia, to the nearest metre.

C. Rod walked 717 m further than Lucia, to the nearest metre.

D. Lucia walked 924 m further than Rod, to the nearest metre.

E. Lucia walked 1174 m further than Rod, to the nearest metre.

[VCAA 2021 FM]

Question 129

$\sin^2\left(\frac{3\pi}{4}\right)+\cos^2\left(\frac{3\pi}{4}\right)$ simplifies to

A. 1 **B.** $\sqrt{2}$ **C.** $\frac{9\pi^2}{8}$ **D.** $\tan^2\left(\frac{3\pi}{4}\right)$ **E.** 0

Question 130

$\frac{1-\cos^2(x)}{\tan(x)}$ simplifies to give

A. $1-\sin^3(x)$

B. $\sin(x)\cos(x)$

C. $1-\cos^3(x)$

D. $(1-\sin(x))(1-\cos(x))$

E. $\frac{1}{\tan(x)}$

Question 131

$\frac{\cos\left(\frac{\pi}{2}-x\right)}{\sin\left(\frac{\pi}{2}-x\right)}$ simplifies to give

A. 1

B. $\cot(x)$

C. $\sin(x)\cos(x)$

D. ∞

E. $\tan(x)$

Question 132

If $\cos(x)=-a$ and $\cot(x)=b$, where $a,b>0$, then $\operatorname{cosec}(-x)$ is equal to

A. $\frac{b}{a}$ **B.** $-\frac{b}{a}$ **C.** $-\frac{a}{b}$ **D.** $\frac{a}{b}$ **E.** $-ab$

[VCAA 2018 SM]

Question 133

The area of a sector of a circle of radius 6 cm is 50 cm^2.

Find the length of the arc of the sector.

Question 134

The diagram shows a circle with centre O and radius 2 cm.

The points A and B lie on the circumference of the circle and $\angle AOB = \theta$.

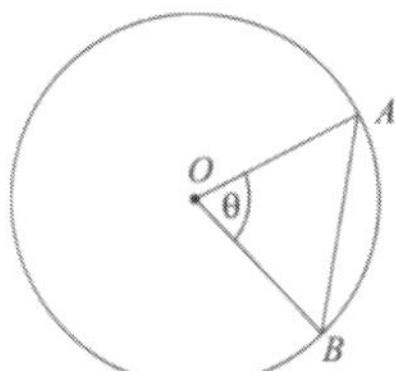

The diagram is not to scale.

a. There are two possible values of θ for which the area of ΔAOB is $\sqrt{3}$ cm^2.

One value is $\frac{\pi}{3}$. Find the other value.

Suppose that $\theta = \frac{\pi}{3}$.

b. Find the area of the sector AOB.

c. Find the exact length of the perimeter of the minor segment bounded by the chord AB and the arc AB.

Question 135

The diagram shows a circle with centre O and radius 5 cm. The length of the arc PQ is 9 cm.

Lines drawn perpendicular to OP and OQ at P and Q respectively meet at T.

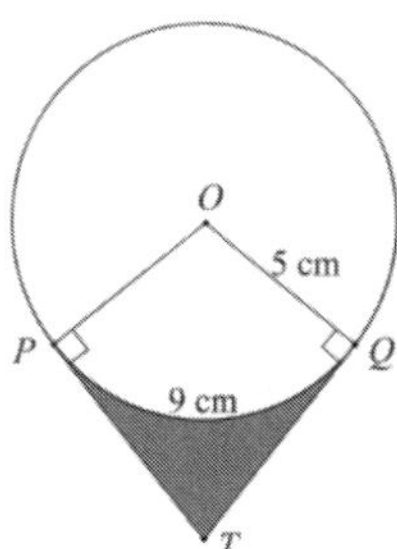

The diagram is not to scale.

a. Find $\angle POQ$ in radians.

b. Prove that ΔOPT is congruent to ΔOQT.

c. Find the length of PT, correct to one decimal place.

d. Find the area of the shaded region, correct to one decimal place.

Question 136

In triangle PQR, $PQ = 8$ cm, $PR = 13$ cm and $\angle PQR = 60°$. Let $QR = x$ cm.

Use the cosine rule to find an equation in x and hence find the length of QR.

Question 137

In ΔABC, $\angle A = 50°$ and $\angle B = 60°$. The perimeter of the triangle is 30 cm.

Find the length of the longest side of the triangle, correct to two decimal places.

Question 138

The diagram below shows a wedge.

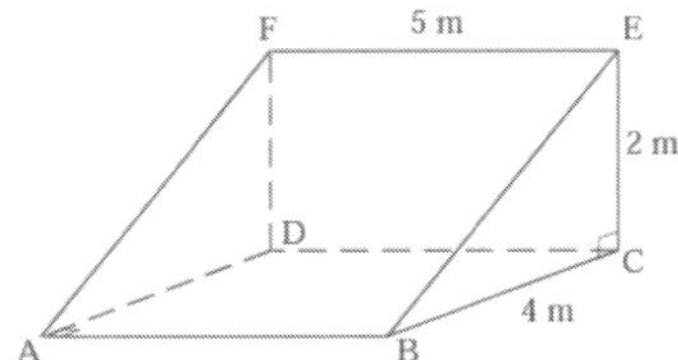

a. Find the angle between the line BE and the plane $ABCD$.

b. Find the angle between the line BF and the plane $ABCD$.

c. Find the angle between the plane $ABCD$ and the plane $ABEF$.

d. Find the angle between the lines BD and BE.

Give all your answers correct to one decimal place.

Question 139

Frank stands at point A on a tennis court and hits two balls.

For Frank's first hit, the ball strikes the ground at point P, 20.7 m from point A.

For Frank's second hit, the ball strikes the ground at point Q.

Point Q is x metres from point A.

Point Q is 10.4 m from point P.

The angle, PAQ, formed is 23.5°.

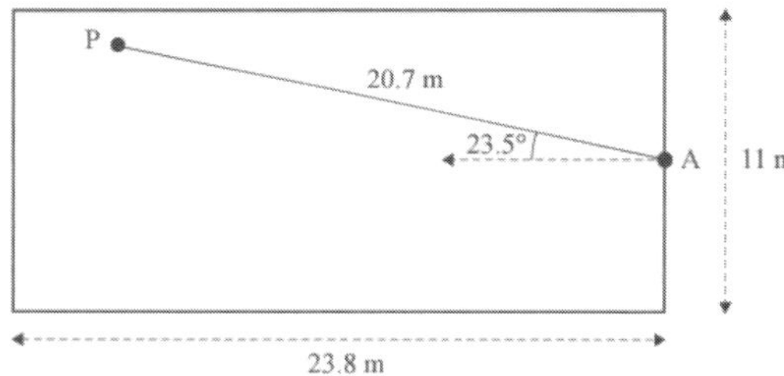

a. Determine two possible values for angle AQP. Round your answers to one decimal place.

b. If point Q is within the boundary court, what is the value of x? Round your answer to the nearest metre.

[VCAA 2018 FM]

Question 140

Simplify the following trigonometric expressions:

a. $\cos^4(\theta)-\sin^4(\theta)$

b. $\dfrac{\sin(2\theta)}{1-\cos^2(\theta)}$

c. $\sin(45°)\cos(45°)$

Question 141

Find the exact value of $\cos(15°)$.

(Hint: Use the $\cos(a-b)$ formula.)

Question 142

Prove the following identities.

a. $\cos(2\theta)+2\sin^2(\theta)=1$

b. $\tan\left(\theta+\frac{\pi}{4}\right)=\frac{1+\tan(\theta)}{1-\tan(\theta)}$

c. $2\sin\left(\theta-\frac{\pi}{6}\right)=\sqrt{3}\sin(\theta)-\cos(\theta)$

d. $\sin(3\theta)=3\sin(\theta)-4\sin^3(\theta)$

(Hint: Use the $\sin(a+b)$ formula to expand $\sin(\theta+2\theta)$.)

Question 143

a. Using $\sin^2(\theta)+\cos^2(\theta)=1$, show that $\operatorname{cosec}^2(\theta)-\cot^2(\theta)=1$.

b. Hence, or otherwise, prove that $\operatorname{cosec}^4(\theta)-\cot^4(\theta)=\operatorname{cosec}^2(\theta)+\cot^2(\theta)$.

c. Solve $\operatorname{cosec}^4(\theta)-\cot^4(\theta)=2-\cot(\theta)$ where $\frac{\pi}{2}<\theta<\pi$.

Question 144

a. Express $4\sin(\theta)+3\cos(\theta)$ in the form $r\cos(\theta-\alpha)$, where r is a positive constant and $0<\alpha<\frac{\pi}{2}$. Give your answer for α in exact form.

b. Hence find the maximum value of $4\sin(\theta)+3\cos(\theta)$ and the smallest positive value of θ for which this maximum occurs. Give your answer for θ in exact form.

The temperature, T°C, of an indoor garden is modelled by

$$T=4\sin\left(\frac{\pi}{12}t\right)+3\cos\left(\frac{\pi}{12}t\right)+15,$$

where t is the time in hours from midday and $0\le t<24$.

c. According to the model, find the minimum temperature of the indoor garden.

d. Find the value of t when this minimum temperature occurs. Give your answer correct to one decimal place.

Question 145

a. Use a products-to-sums identity to prove that $2\sin(x)(\cos(2x)+\cos(4x)+\cos(6x))=\sin(7x)-\sin(x)$.

b. Deduce that $\cos\left(\frac{2\pi}{7}\right)+\cos\left(\frac{4\pi}{7}\right)+\cos\left(\frac{6\pi}{7}\right)=-\frac{1}{2}$.

c. Hence find the value of $\cos\left(\frac{\pi}{7}\right)+\cos\left(\frac{3\pi}{7}\right)+\cos\left(\frac{5\pi}{7}\right)$.

B3. Transformations

Question 146

The translation matrix that maps $P\left(3,-\sqrt{2}\right)$ onto $P\left(-\sqrt{3},-\sqrt{2}\right)$ is

A. $\begin{bmatrix}-1\\0\end{bmatrix}$ **B.** $\begin{bmatrix}-1\\1\end{bmatrix}$ **C.** $\begin{bmatrix}0\\-2\sqrt{2}\end{bmatrix}$ **D.** $\begin{bmatrix}-2\sqrt{3}\\0\end{bmatrix}$ **E.** $\begin{bmatrix}2\sqrt{3}\\0\end{bmatrix}$

Question 147

The transformation given by the matrix $\begin{bmatrix}\frac{\sqrt{3}}{2} & -\frac{1}{2}\\ \frac{1}{2} & \frac{\sqrt{3}}{2}\end{bmatrix}$ is

A. a rotation of $30°$ about the origin

B. a rotation of $60°$ about the origin

C. a reflection in the x-axis

D. a reflection in the y-axis

E. a dilation

Question 148

Under the transformation given by the matrix $\begin{bmatrix}\frac{1}{2} & -\frac{\sqrt{3}}{2}\\ \frac{\sqrt{3}}{2} & \frac{1}{2}\end{bmatrix}$, the image of the point with coordinates $(2,0)$ is

A. $\left(\frac{1}{2},-\frac{\sqrt{3}}{2}\right)$ **B.** $\left(1,-\sqrt{3}\right)$ **C.** $\left(1,\sqrt{3}\right)$ **D.** $\left(\sqrt{3},1\right)$ **E.** $\left(\frac{1}{2},\frac{\sqrt{3}}{2}\right)$

Question 149

In the diagram the square $OPQR$ is mapped onto the parallelogram $OPQ'R'$ by the transformation represented by the matrix

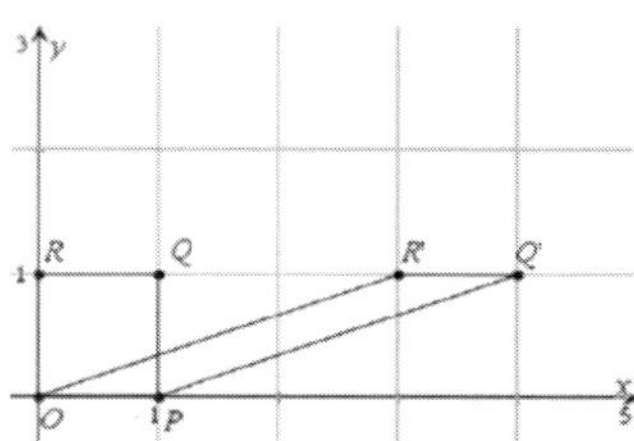

A. $\begin{bmatrix}3 & 0\\0 & 1\end{bmatrix}$ **B.** $\begin{bmatrix}0 & 3\\0 & 0\end{bmatrix}$ **C.** $\begin{bmatrix}1 & 3\\0 & 1\end{bmatrix}$ **D.** $\begin{bmatrix}1 & 0\\3 & 1\end{bmatrix}$ **E.** $\begin{bmatrix}3 & 0\\0 & 3\end{bmatrix}$

Question 150

Graph R is rotated about the origin to produce graph S.

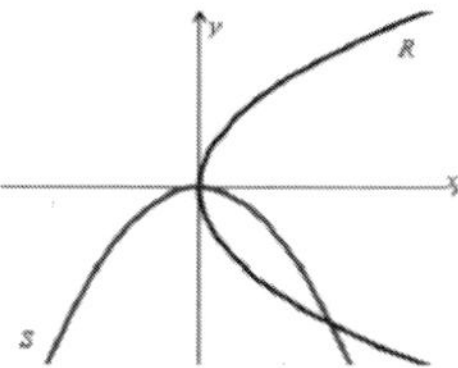

The matrix for this transformation is

A. $\begin{bmatrix} -1 & 0 \\ 0 & -1 \end{bmatrix}$ **B.** $\begin{bmatrix} 0 & 1 \\ -1 & 0 \end{bmatrix}$ **C.** $\begin{bmatrix} 0 & 1 \\ 1 & 0 \end{bmatrix}$ **D.** $\begin{bmatrix} 0 & -1 \\ -1 & 0 \end{bmatrix}$ **E.** $\begin{bmatrix} 0 & -1 \\ 1 & 0 \end{bmatrix}$

Question 151

P is the point $(-1,2)$.

If P is subject to a dilation by a factor of 3 units in the y direction, followed by a translation of $\begin{bmatrix} 2 \\ 1 \end{bmatrix}$, then the coordinates of the image of P are

A. $(-1,7)$ **B.** $(-1,3)$ **C.** $(0,8)$ **D.** $(1,7)$ **E.** $(1,9)$

Question 152

The matrix that represents an anticlockwise rotation about the origin of $90°$ is

A. $\begin{bmatrix} 0 & -1 \\ 1 & 0 \end{bmatrix}$ **B.** $\begin{bmatrix} 0 & 1 \\ -1 & 0 \end{bmatrix}$ **C.** $\begin{bmatrix} 1 & -1 \\ 1 & 1 \end{bmatrix}$ **D.** $\begin{bmatrix} 1 & 0 \\ 0 & 1 \end{bmatrix}$ **E.** $\begin{bmatrix} -1 & 0 \\ 0 & -1 \end{bmatrix}$

Question 153

The rectangle with vertices (0,0), (0,2), (3,2) and (3,0) is changed under a linear transformation whose matrix is $\begin{bmatrix} 1 & -1 \\ 1 & 1 \end{bmatrix}$.

The area of its image is

A. 0 **B.** 3 **C.** 6 **D.** 12 **E.** 24

Question 154

The line with equation $y = 2x + 1$ undergoes dilation by a factor of 2 units parallel to the x-axis.

The image is a line with equation

A. $y = x + \frac{1}{2}$

B. $y = x + 1$

C. $y = 2x - 1$

D. $y = 4x + 1$

E. $y = 4x + 2$

Question 155

The smaller square is transformed into the larger square.

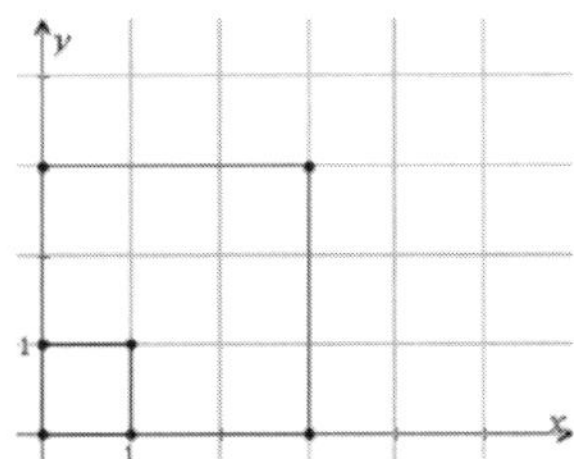

If the matrix associated with this transformation is $\begin{bmatrix} a & b \\ c & d \end{bmatrix}$, then $ad - bc$ equals

A. $\frac{1}{3}$ **B.** 3 **C.** 6 **D.** 9 **E.** $\frac{1}{9}$

Question 156

A composite transformation consists of a reflection in the x-axis followed by a rotation defined by the matrix $\frac{1}{2}\begin{bmatrix} 1 & -\sqrt{3} \\ \sqrt{3} & 1 \end{bmatrix}$.

The matrix of the composite transformation is

A. $\frac{1}{2}\begin{bmatrix} -\sqrt{3} & 1 \\ 1 & \sqrt{3} \end{bmatrix}$ **B.** $\frac{1}{2}\begin{bmatrix} 1 & \sqrt{3} \\ \sqrt{3} & -1 \end{bmatrix}$ **C.** $\frac{1}{2}\begin{bmatrix} 1 & -\sqrt{3} \\ -\sqrt{3} & -1 \end{bmatrix}$

D. $\frac{1}{2}\begin{bmatrix} -1 & -\sqrt{3} \\ -\sqrt{3} & 1 \end{bmatrix}$ **E.** $\frac{1}{2}\begin{bmatrix} -1 & \sqrt{3} \\ \sqrt{3} & 1 \end{bmatrix}$

Question 157

For each of the following matrix transformations which operate on the graph of $y = x^2$, state the equation of the image of $y = x^2$ and write down the type of transformation that has taken place.

a. $\begin{bmatrix} 1 \\ -2 \end{bmatrix}$

b. $\begin{bmatrix} 1 & 0 \\ 0 & 4 \end{bmatrix}$

c. $\begin{bmatrix} 1 & 0 \\ 0 & -1 \end{bmatrix}$

d. $\begin{bmatrix} 0 & 1 \\ -1 & 0 \end{bmatrix}$

Question 158

Determine the nature of each of the following transformations:

a. $(x, y) \rightarrow \left(\frac{1}{5}(-3x - 4y), \frac{1}{5}(-4x + 3y)\right)$.

b. $(x, y) \rightarrow \left(\frac{1}{5}(3x - 4y), \frac{1}{5}(4x + 3y)\right)$.

Question 159

Find the equation of the image of the line $y = 2x - 1$ under a reflection in the line $y = -x$ followed by an anticlockwise rotation of $\frac{3\pi}{4}$ about O. Give your answer in the form $ax + by = c$ where $a, b, c \in R$.

Question 160

The triangle T_1 is mapped by the matrix $M = \begin{bmatrix} 4 & -1 \\ 3 & 1 \end{bmatrix}$ to a triangle T_2.

The vertices of T_2 have coordinates $P_2(4,3)$, $Q_2(4,10)$ and $R_2(16,12)$.

a. Find the coordinates of the vertices of T_1.

b. Find the area of T_1.

c. Hence, use the determinant of M to find the area of T_2.

B4. Vectors in the plane

Question 161

If $\underset{\sim}{a} = \begin{bmatrix} 1 \\ -2 \end{bmatrix}$ and $\underset{\sim}{b} = \begin{bmatrix} -3 \\ 1 \end{bmatrix}$, then $3\underset{\sim}{a} - \underset{\sim}{b}$ is equal to

A. $\begin{bmatrix} 0 \\ -7 \end{bmatrix}$ **B.** $\begin{bmatrix} 0 \\ -5 \end{bmatrix}$ **C.** $\begin{bmatrix} 6 \\ -7 \end{bmatrix}$ **D.** $\begin{bmatrix} 6 \\ -5 \end{bmatrix}$ **E.** $\begin{bmatrix} 6 \\ 7 \end{bmatrix}$

Question 162

If $\overrightarrow{OA} = 3\underset{\sim}{i} - \underset{\sim}{j}$ and $\overrightarrow{OB} = -\underset{\sim}{i} + 2\underset{\sim}{j}$, then $\overrightarrow{AB}$ is

A. $2\underset{\sim}{i} - \underset{\sim}{j}$ **B.** $-2\underset{\sim}{i} + \underset{\sim}{j}$ **C.** $-2\underset{\sim}{i} + 3\underset{\sim}{j}$ **D.** $-4\underset{\sim}{i} + \underset{\sim}{j}$ **E.** $-4\underset{\sim}{i} + 3\underset{\sim}{j}$

Question 163

A unit vector in the direction of $3\underset{\sim}{i} - 2\underset{\sim}{j}$ is equal to

A. $\frac{1}{13}(3\underset{\sim}{i} - 2\underset{\sim}{j})$ **B.** $\frac{1}{5}(3\underset{\sim}{i} - 2\underset{\sim}{j})$ **C.** $\frac{1}{\sqrt{13}}(3\underset{\sim}{i} - 2\underset{\sim}{j})$ **D.** $\frac{1}{\sqrt{5}}(3\underset{\sim}{i} - 2\underset{\sim}{j})$ **E.** $-\frac{1}{\sqrt{13}}(3\underset{\sim}{i} - 2\underset{\sim}{j})$

Question 164

The two distinct points P and Q have non-zero position vectors $\underset{\sim}{p}$ and $\underset{\sim}{q}$ respectively.

Consider a third point R. The vector from Q to R is $3\underset{\sim}{i} + \underset{\sim}{j}$.

Which one of the following would mean that P, Q and R lie in a straight line?

A. $\underset{\sim}{p} - \underset{\sim}{q} = \underset{\sim}{i} + \underset{\sim}{j}$

B. $p = 3$ and $q = 1$

C. $-\underset{\sim}{p} + \underset{\sim}{q} = 6\underset{\sim}{i} + 2\underset{\sim}{j}$

D. $\underset{\sim}{p} + \underset{\sim}{q} = \underset{\sim}{0}$

E. $-\underset{\sim}{p} + \underset{\sim}{q} \neq \underset{\sim}{0}$

Question 165

Which of the following are pairs of perpendicular unit vectors?

A. $\underset{\sim}{i}$ and $2\underset{\sim}{j}$

B. $\underset{\sim}{i} + \underset{\sim}{j}$ and $\underset{\sim}{i} - \underset{\sim}{j}$

C. $\frac{1}{\sqrt{2}}\underset{\sim}{i} - \frac{1}{\sqrt{2}}\underset{\sim}{j}$ and $-\frac{1}{\sqrt{2}}\underset{\sim}{i} + \frac{1}{\sqrt{2}}\underset{\sim}{j}$

D. $\frac{1}{\sqrt{2}}\underset{\sim}{i} - \frac{1}{\sqrt{2}}\underset{\sim}{j}$ and $\frac{1}{\sqrt{2}}\underset{\sim}{i} + \frac{1}{\sqrt{2}}\underset{\sim}{j}$

E. $\frac{1}{\sqrt{2}}\underset{\sim}{i} - \frac{1}{\sqrt{2}}\underset{\sim}{j}$ and $\sqrt{2}\underset{\sim}{i} + \sqrt{2}\underset{\sim}{j}$

B4. Vectors in the plane

Question 166

The scalar resolute of vector $\underset{\sim}{a}$ in the direction of vector $\underset{\sim}{b}$ is -4.

If $\underset{\sim}{b} = -\sqrt{3}\underset{\sim}{i}$, the vector resolute of $\underset{\sim}{a}$ in the direction of $\underset{\sim}{b}$ is

A. $-4\underset{\sim}{i}$ **B.** $-3\underset{\sim}{i}$ **C.** $\frac{1}{\sqrt{3}}\underset{\sim}{i}$ **D.** $3\underset{\sim}{i}$ **E.** $4\underset{\sim}{i}$

[VCAA 2021 SM]

Question 167

Consider the vectors $\underset{\sim}{a} = x\underset{\sim}{i} + \underset{\sim}{j}$, $\underset{\sim}{b} = \underset{\sim}{i} - \underset{\sim}{j}$ and $\underset{\sim}{c} = \underset{\sim}{i} + x\underset{\sim}{j}$.

Given that θ is the angle between $\underset{\sim}{a}$ and $\underset{\sim}{b}$, and ϕ is the angle between $\underset{\sim}{b}$ and $\underset{\sim}{c}$, $\cos(\theta)\cos(\phi)$ is

A. $\frac{2(1+x^2)}{1-x^2}$ **B.** $\frac{\sqrt{2}(1-x^2)}{1+x^2}$ **C.** $-\frac{(x+1)^2}{2(1+x^2)}$ **D.** $-\frac{(x-1)^2}{2(1+x^2)}$ **E.** $\frac{\sqrt{2}(1+x^2)}{1-x^2}$

[VCAA 2021 SM]

Question 168

If $|\underset{\sim}{a} + \underset{\sim}{b}| = |\underset{\sim}{a}| + |\underset{\sim}{b}|$ and $\underset{\sim}{a}, \underset{\sim}{b} \neq \underset{\sim}{0}$, which one of the following is **necessarily true**?

A. $\underset{\sim}{a}$ is parallel to $\underset{\sim}{b}$

B. $|\underset{\sim}{a}| = |\underset{\sim}{b}|$

C. $\underset{\sim}{a} = \underset{\sim}{b}$

D. $\underset{\sim}{a} = -\underset{\sim}{b}$

E. $\underset{\sim}{a}$ is perpendicular to $\underset{\sim}{b}$

[VCAA 2018 SM]

Question 169

A body has displacement of $3\underset{\sim}{i} + \underset{\sim}{j}$ metres at a particular time. The body moves with constant velocity and two seconds later its displacement is $-\underset{\sim}{i} + 5\underset{\sim}{j}$ metres.

The velocity, in ms^{-1}, of the body is

A. $2\underset{\sim}{i} + 6\underset{\sim}{j}$ **B.** $-2\underset{\sim}{i} + 2\underset{\sim}{j}$ **C.** $-4\underset{\sim}{i} + 4\underset{\sim}{j}$ **D.** $4\underset{\sim}{i} - 4\underset{\sim}{j}$ **E.** $\underset{\sim}{i} + 3\underset{\sim}{j}$

[VCAA 2017 SM]

Question 170

The component of the force $\underset{\sim}{F} = a\underset{\sim}{i} + b\underset{\sim}{j}$, where a and b are non-zero constants, in the direction of the vector $\underset{\sim}{w} = \underset{\sim}{i} + \underset{\sim}{j}$, is

A. $\left(\frac{a+b}{2}\right)\underset{\sim}{w}$ **B.** $\frac{\underset{\sim}{F}}{a+b}$ **C.** $\left(\frac{a+b}{a^2+b^2}\right)\underset{\sim}{F}$ **D.** $(a+b)\underset{\sim}{w}$ **E.** $\left(\frac{a+b}{\sqrt{2}}\right)\underset{\sim}{w}$

[VCAA 2015 SM]

Question 171

A stationary particle is acted on by three forces, $\underset{\sim}{A}$, $\underset{\sim}{B}$ and $\underset{\sim}{C}$. Force $\underset{\sim}{A}$ has magnitude 10 newtons and acts due west.

Force $\underset{\sim}{B}$ has magnitude 10 newtons and acts due north.

The magnitude and direction of force $\underset{\sim}{C}$ are, respectively

A. 10 newtons, southwest

B. $10\sqrt{2}$ newtons, southeast

C. $10\sqrt{2}$ newtons, northwest

D. 20 newtons, southeast

E. 10 newtons, northwest

Question 172

The diagram below shows a stationary body being acted on by four forces whose magnitudes are in newtons.

The force of magnitude F_1 newtons acts in the opposite direction to the force of magnitude 8 N.

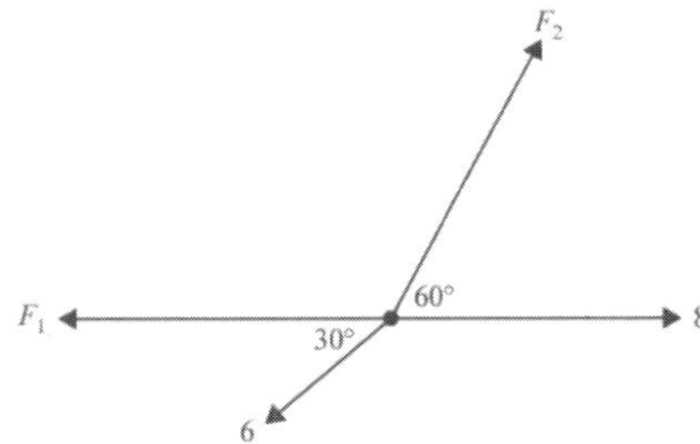

The value of F_1 is

A. $8-2\sqrt{3}$ **B.** $2\sqrt{3}$ **C.** 8 **D.** $8+2\sqrt{3}$ **E.** $8-3\sqrt{3}$

[VCAA 2021 SM]

Question 173

Consider triangle *ABC* and let *M* and *N* be the midpoints of *AC* and *BC* respectively.

Prove that the line segment joining the midpoints of two sides of *ABC* is parallel to the third side and half its length.

Question 174

OACB is a parallelogram with $\overrightarrow{OA} = \underset{\sim}{a}$ and $\overrightarrow{OB} = \underset{\sim}{b}$.

a. Show that $\left|\overrightarrow{OC}\right|^2 = a^2 + 2\underset{\sim}{a}\cdot\underset{\sim}{b} + b^2$.

b. Show that $\left|\overrightarrow{AB}\right|^2 = b^2 - 2\underset{\sim}{a}\cdot\underset{\sim}{b} + a^2$.

c. Hence prove that if OC and AB are equal in length, then *OACB* is a rectangle.

Question 175

Let $\underset{\sim}{v} = a\underset{\sim}{i} + \underset{\sim}{j}$ and $\underset{\sim}{w} = -\underset{\sim}{i} + a\underset{\sim}{j}$, where $a \in R$. The angle between $\underset{\sim}{v}$ and $\underset{\sim}{w}$ is $30°$.

Find in exact form the possible values of *a*.

Question 176

Let $\underset{\sim}{i}$ and $\underset{\sim}{j}$ be unit vectors in the east and north directions respectively.

Kate leaves her base camp and walks on flat terrain for 4 km in a NE direction. She then walks a further 6 km on a true bearing of $300°$.

If she then walks directly back to her base camp, find an expression in exact form in terms of $\underset{\sim}{i}$ and $\underset{\sim}{j}$ for the vector that describes her final path.

Question 177

A boat *A* is moving with velocity $\left(5\underset{\sim}{i} - 4\underset{\sim}{j}\right)$ kmh^{-1} and a boat *B* is moving with velocity $\left(3\underset{\sim}{i} + 7\underset{\sim}{j}\right)$ kmh^{-1}.

Find the direction that boat *B* appears to be moving in, to an observer on boat *A*, giving your answer as a bearing.

Note: In this question, $\underset{\sim}{i}$ and $\underset{\sim}{j}$ are unit vectors due east and north respectively.

Question 178

Cadel cycles at a constant speed u ms^{-1} on horizontal ground and finds that when his velocity is $u\underset{\sim}{j}$ ms^{-1} the velocity of the wind appears to be $c\left(3\underset{\sim}{i}-4\underset{\sim}{j}\right)$ ms^{-1}, where c is a positive constant.

When Cadel cycles with velocity $\frac{1}{5}u\left(-3\underset{\sim}{i}+4\underset{\sim}{j}\right)$ ms^{-1}, the velocity of the wind appears to be $k\underset{\sim}{i}$ ms^{-1}, where k is a positive constant.

Find, in terms of u, the true velocity of the wind, $\underset{\sim}{v}$.

Note: In this question, $\underset{\sim}{i}$ and $\underset{\sim}{j}$ are unit vectors due east and north respectively.

Question 179

A particle of mass 3 kg moves under the action of two constant forces $\left(6\underset{\sim}{i}+2\underset{\sim}{j}\right)$ N and $\left(3\underset{\sim}{i}-5\underset{\sim}{j}\right)$ N.

a. Find the resultant force $\underset{\sim}{F}$ acting on the particle.

b. Find the angle between $\underset{\sim}{F}$ and $\underset{\sim}{j}$. Give your answer in degrees correct to one decimal place.

c. Find the acceleration of the particle, giving your answer as a vector.

d. The initial velocity of the particle is $\left(-2\underset{\sim}{i}+\underset{\sim}{j}\right)$ ms^{-1}. Find the exact speed of the particle after 2 seconds.

Question 180

A body of mass 10 kg is held in place on a smooth plane inclined at $30°$ to the horizontal by a tension force, T newtons, acting parallel to the plane.

a. On the diagram below, show all other forces acting on the body and label them.

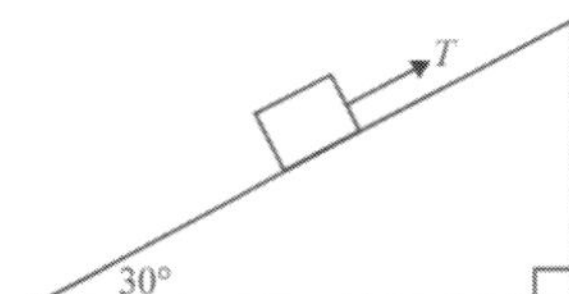

b. Find the value of T.

[VCAA 2013 SM]

B5. Complex numbers

Use the following information for questions 181–183.

Let $a = 1 + i$, $b = 2 - 3i$ and $c = -i$.

Question 181

The expression $a + 2b - c$ is equal to

A. $-5 + 4i$ **B.** $5 - 4i$ **C.** $5 - 6i$ **D.** $2 + 3i$ **E.** $3 - 3i$

Question 182

b^2 is equal to

A. $4 - 9i$ **B.** $4 + 12i$ **C.** $-5 - 12i$ **D.** 9 **E.** -5

Question 183

abc is equal to

A. $-3i$ **B.** -1 **C.** $1 + 5i$ **D.** $3 - 4i$ **E.** $-1 - 5i$

Question 184

The factorised form of $z^2 - 4z + 8$ is

A. $(z - 2 \pm 2i)^2$

B. $(z + 2 + 2i)(z + 2 - 2i)$

C. $(z - 2 + 2i)(z - 2 - 2i)$

D. $(z + 2 - 2i)(z - 2 + 2i)$

E. $(z + 2 + 2i)(z - 2 - 2i)$

Question 185

Let $z = a + bi$, where $a, b \in R \setminus \{0\}$.

If $z + \frac{1}{z} \in R$, which one of the following must be **true**?

A. $\text{Arg}(z) = \frac{\pi}{4}$

B. $a = -b$

C. $a = b$

D. $|z| = 1$

E. $z^2 = 1$

[VCAA 2018 SM]

Question 186

The expression $i^{1!} + i^{2!} + i^{3!} + ... + i^{100!}$ is equal to

A. 0 **B.** 96 **C.** $95 + i$ **D.** $94 + 2i$ **E.** $98 + 2i$

[VCAA 2019 SM]

B5. Complex numbers

Question 187

Given the complex number $z = a+bi$, where $a \in R\setminus\{0\}$ and $b \in R$, $\dfrac{4z\bar{z}}{(z+\bar{z})^2}$ is equivalent to

A. $1+\left(\dfrac{\text{Im}(z)}{\text{Re}(z)}\right)^2$ **B.** $4[\text{Re}(z)\times\text{Im}(z)]$ **C.** $4\left([\text{Re}(z)]^2+[\text{Im}(z)]^2\right)$

D. $4\left[1+(\text{Re}(z)+\text{Im}(z))^2\right]$ **E.** $\dfrac{2\times\text{Im}(z)}{[\text{Re}(z)]^2}$

[VCAA 2020 SM]

Question 188

Given that $(x+iy)^{14} = a+ib$, where $x, y, a, b \in R$, $(y-ix)^{14}$ for all values of x and y is equal to

A. $-a-ib$ **B.** $b-ia$ **C.** $-b+ia$ **D.** $-a+ib$ **E.** $b+ia$

[VCAA 2020 SM]

Question 189

If $z=-2i$, then $|z^2|$ and $\text{Arg}(z^2)$ are respectively

A. 2 and π **B.** 4 and π **C.** 4 and $-\pi$ **D.** -4 and 0 **E.** -4 and π

Use the following information for questions 190–192.

Let $w = 2\text{cis}\left(\dfrac{\pi}{6}\right)$, $v = \text{cis}\left(\dfrac{\pi}{4}\right)$ and $z = 3\text{cis}\left(\dfrac{\pi}{3}\right)$.

Question 190

The expression $\dfrac{z}{v}$ is equal to

A. $\dfrac{1}{3}\text{cis}\left(-\dfrac{\pi}{12}\right)$ **B.** $3\text{cis}\left(-\dfrac{\pi}{12}\right)$ **C.** $3\text{cis}\left(\dfrac{\pi}{12}\right)$ **D.** $\dfrac{1}{3}\text{cis}\left(\dfrac{\pi}{12}\right)$ **E.** $\dfrac{1}{3}\text{cis}\left(-\dfrac{2\pi}{7}\right)$

Question 191

The expression w^7 is equal to

A. $14\text{cis}\left(\dfrac{\pi}{30}\right)$ **B.** $14\text{cis}\left(\dfrac{5\pi}{6}\right)$ **C.** $128\text{cis}\left(\dfrac{5\pi}{6}\right)$ **D.** $128\text{cis}\left(\dfrac{5+\pi}{6}\right)$ **E.** $128\text{cis}\left(-\dfrac{5\pi}{6}\right)$

Question 192

The expression w^2v is equal to

A. $4\text{cis}\left(\dfrac{2\pi}{7}\right)$ **B.** $4\text{cis}\left(\dfrac{7\pi}{12}\right)$ **C.** $2\text{cis}\left(\dfrac{7\pi}{12}\right)$ **D.** $4\text{cis}\left(\dfrac{7\pi}{6}\right)$ **E.** $4\text{cis}\left(\dfrac{\pi}{6}\right)$

Question 193

For $z \in C$, if $\text{Im}(z) > 0$ then $\text{Arg}\left(\dfrac{z\bar{z}}{z-\bar{z}}\right)$ is

A. $-\dfrac{\pi}{2}$ **B.** 0 **C.** $\dfrac{\pi}{4}$ **D.** $\dfrac{\pi}{2}$ **E.** π

[VCAA 2021 SM]

Question 194

The complex numbers z, iz and $z+iz$, where $z \in C\setminus\{0\}$, are plotted in the Argand plane, forming the vertices of a triangle.

The area of this triangle is given by

A. $|z|$ **B.** $|z|+|z|^2$ **C.** $\dfrac{|z|^2}{2}$ **D.** $|z|^2$ **E.** $\dfrac{\sqrt{3}|z|^2}{2}$

[VCAA 2018 SM]

Question 195

Let $z = x + yi$, where $x, y \in R$. The rays $\operatorname{Arg}(z-2) = \frac{\pi}{4}$ and $\operatorname{Arg}(z-(5+i)) = \frac{5\pi}{6}$, where $z \in C$, intersect on the complex plane at a point (a,b).

The value of b is

A. $-\sqrt{3}$ **B.** $2-\sqrt{3}$ **C.** 0 **D.** $\sqrt{3}$ **E.** $2+\sqrt{3}$

[VCAA 2019 SM]

Question 196

The graph of the circle given by $\left|z-2-\sqrt{3}i\right| = 1$, where $z \in C$, is shown below.

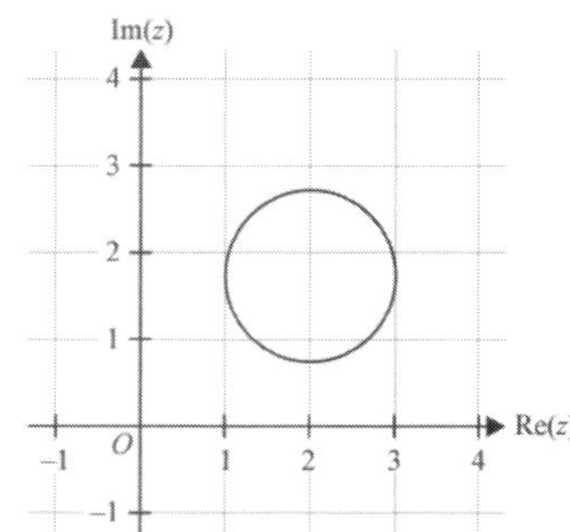

For points on this circle, the maximum value of $|z|$ is

A. $\sqrt{3}+1$ **B.** 3 **C.** $\sqrt{13}$ **D.** $\sqrt{7}+1$ **E.** 8

[VCAA 2021 SM]

Question 197

a. Solve $z^2 + 2z + 2 = 0$ for z, where $z \in C$.

b. Solve $z^2 + 2\bar{z} + 2 = 0$ for z, where $z \in C$.

[VCAA 2021 SM]

Question 198

a. Show that the solutions of $2z^2 + 4z + 5 = 0$, where $z \in C$, are $z = -1 \pm \frac{\sqrt{6}}{2}i$.

b. Plot the solutions of $2z^2 + 4z + 5 = 0$ on the Argand diagram below.

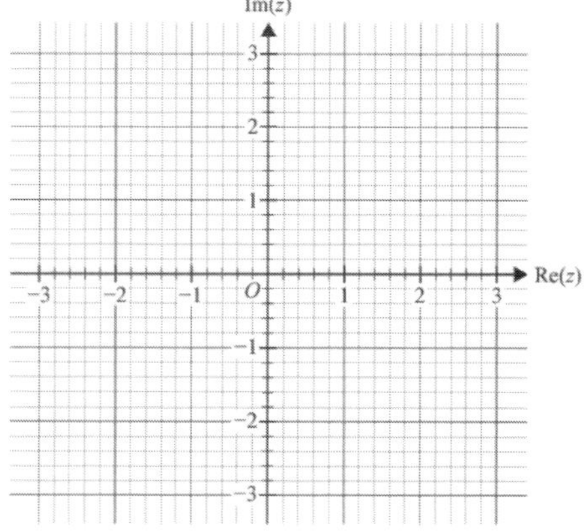

Let $|z+m|=n$, where $m, n \in R$, represent the circle of minimum radius that passes through the solutions of $2z^2+4z+5=0$.

c. Find the value of m and the value of n.

d. Find the cartesian equation of the circle $|z+m|=n$.

e. Sketch the circle on the Argand diagram in **part b**. Intercepts with the coordinate axes do not need to be calculated or labelled.

f. Find all values of d, where $d \in R$, for which the solutions of $2z^2+4z+d=0$ satisfy the relation $|z+m| \le n$.

g. All complex solutions of $az^2+bz+c=0$ have non-zero real and imaginary parts. Let $|z+p|=q$ represent the circle of minimum radius in the complex plane that passes through these solutions, where $a, b, c, p, q \in R$.

Find p and q in terms of a, b and c.

[VCAA 2019 SM]

Question 199

Two complex numbers, u and v, are defined as $u=-2-i$ and $v=-4-3i$.

a. Express the relation $|z-u|=|z-v|$ in the cartesian form $y=mx+c$, where $m, c \in R$.

b. Plot the points that represent u and v and the relation $|z-u|=|z-v|$ on the Argand diagram below.

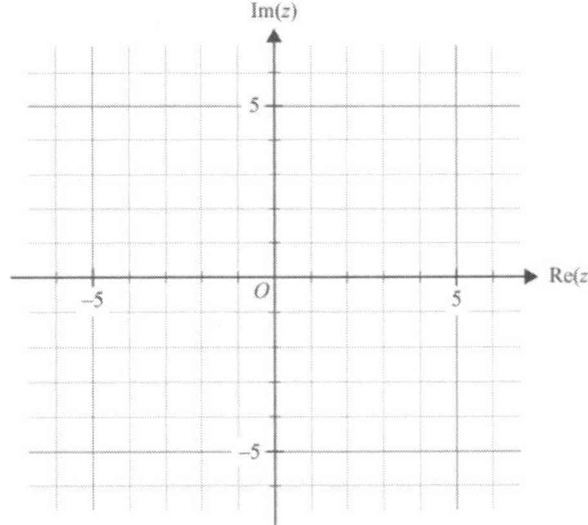

c. State a geometrical interpretation of the graph of $|z-u|=|z-v|$ in relation to the points that represent u and v.

d. Sketch the ray given by $\text{Arg}(z-u)=\frac{\pi}{4}$ on the Argand diagram in **part b**.

e. Write down the function that describes the ray $\text{Arg}(z-u)=\frac{\pi}{4}$, giving the rule in cartesian form.

f. The points representing u and v and $-5i$ lie on the circle given by $|z-z_c|=r$, where z_c is the centre of the circle and r is the radius.

Find z_c in the form $a+ib$ where $a, b \in R$, and find the radius r.

[VCAA 2020 SM]

Question 200

Consider the point $z_4 = \sqrt{3} + i$.

a. Sketch the ray given by $\text{Arg}(z - z_4) = \dfrac{5\pi}{6}$ on the Argand diagram below.

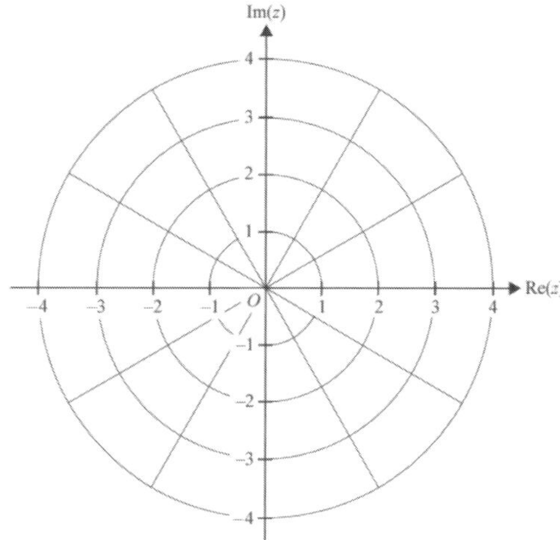

The ray $\text{Arg}(z - z_4) = \dfrac{5\pi}{6}$ intersects the circle $|z - 3i| = 1$, dividing it into a major and a minor segment.

b. Sketch the circle $|z - 3i| = 1$ on the Argand diagram in **part a**.

c. Find the area of the minor segment.

[VCAA 2021 SM]

B6. Functions, relations and graphs

Question 201

The algebraic fraction $\dfrac{7x-5}{(x-4)^2(x^2+9)}$ could be expressed in partial fraction form as

A. $\dfrac{A}{(x-4)^2}+\dfrac{B}{x^2+9}$

B. $\dfrac{A}{x-4}+\dfrac{B}{x-3}+\dfrac{C}{x+3}$

C. $\dfrac{A}{(x-4)^2}+\dfrac{Bx+C}{x^2+9}$

D. $\dfrac{A}{x-4}+\dfrac{B}{(x-4)^2}+\dfrac{Cx+D}{x^2+9}$

E. $\dfrac{A}{x-4}+\dfrac{B}{(x-4)^2}+\dfrac{C}{x^2+9}$

[VCAA 2016 Sample SM]

Question 202

The implied domain of the function with rule $f(x)=1-\sec\left(x+\dfrac{\pi}{4}\right)$ is

A. R

B. $[0,2]$

C. $R\backslash\left\{\dfrac{(4n-1)\pi}{4}\right\},\ n\in Z$

D. $R\backslash\left\{\dfrac{(4n+1)\pi}{4}\right\},\ n\in Z$

E. $R\backslash\left\{\dfrac{(2n-1)\pi}{2}\right\},\ n\in Z$

[VCAA 2019 SM]

Question 203

The domain of $\arcsin(2x-1)$ is

A. $[-1,1]$

B. $[-1,0]$

C. $[0,1]$

D. $\left[-\dfrac{1}{2},\dfrac{1}{2}\right]$

E. $\left[0,\dfrac{1}{2}\right]$

[VCAA 2014 SM]

Question 204

Part of the graph of $y=\frac{1}{2}\tan^{-1}(x)$ is shown below.

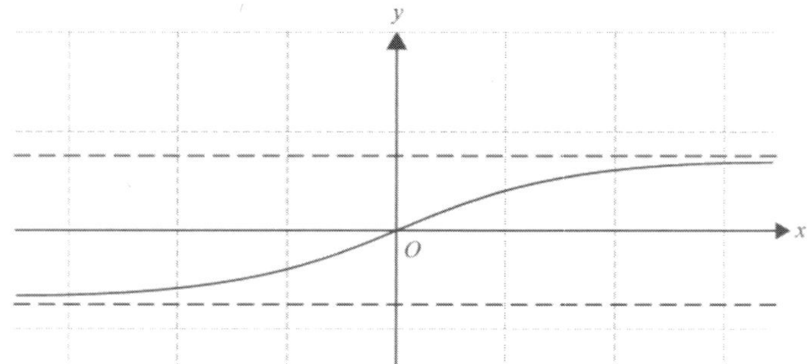

The equations of its asymptotes are

A. $y=\pm\frac{1}{2}$ **B.** $y=\pm\frac{3}{4}$ **C.** $y=\pm 1$ **D.** $y=\pm\frac{\pi}{2}$ **E.** $y=\pm\frac{\pi}{4}$

[VCAA 2018 SM]

Question 205

Let A be the point $(-2,1)$ and B the point $(0,-3)$.

The locus of points $P(x,y)$ for which $AP=BP$ has equation

A. $x-2y=-3$ **B.** $x-2y=1$ **C.** $x+2y=1$ **D.** $x+2y=-1$ **E.** $x+2y=-3$

Question 206

The locus of points $P(x,y)$ that are equidistant from the point $(0,-a)$ and the line $y=a$ is a parabola with equation

A. $y=2ax^2$ **B.** $y=4ax^2$ **C.** $y=-4ax^2$ **D.** $y=\frac{1}{4a}x^2$ **E.** $y=-\frac{1}{4a}x^2$

Question 207

The curve with equation $4x^2+8y^2=2$ is

A. an ellipse

B. a parabola

C. a rectangular hyperbola

D. a non-rectangular hyperbola

E. a circle

Question 208

A curve C can be represented by the parametric equations $x=1+t$ and $y=1-t$.

The cartesian equation of C is

A. $y=x-2$ **B.** $y=x+2$ **C.** $y=-x-2$ **D.** $y=-x+2$ **E.** $y=x-1$

Question 209

Consider the hyperbola with equation $\frac{x^2}{9}-y^2=1$.

This hyperbola has asymptotes

A. $y=\pm 3x$ **B.** $y=2x+3$ **C.** $y=\pm\frac{3}{x}$ **D.** $y=3x$ **E.** $y=\pm\frac{x}{3}$

Question 210

The cartesian point $\left(\sqrt{3},-1\right)$ expressed in polar form is

A. $[2,-30°]$ **B.** $[2,30°]$ **C.** $[-2,-30°]$ **D.** $[4,-60°]$ **E.** $[4,60°]$

Question 211

The polar coordinates $[3,120°]$ specify the same point as the cartesian coordinates

A. $\left(-\frac{3\sqrt{3}}{2},\frac{3}{2}\right)$ **B.** $\left(-\frac{3}{2},\frac{3\sqrt{3}}{2}\right)$ **C.** $\left(\frac{3}{2},-\frac{3\sqrt{3}}{2}\right)$ **D.** $\left(-\frac{1}{2},\frac{\sqrt{3}}{2}\right)$ **E.** $\left(-\frac{3}{2},-\frac{3\sqrt{3}}{2}\right)$

Question 212

The polar coordinates $[-2,20°]$ specify the same point as

A. $[2,20°]$ **B.** $[2,-20°]$ **C.** $[2,160°]$ **D.** $[2,200°]$ **E.** $[2,340°]$

Question 213

Converting the polar equation $r=\frac{1}{1-\sin(\theta)}$, $\sin(\theta)\neq 1$ into cartesian form gives the equation

A. $y^2=1+2y$ **B.** $y=\frac{1}{2}\left(x^2-1\right)$ **C.** $y=\pm\left(1-x^2\right)$

D. $y=\pm\left(1-x^2\right)+1$ **E.** $y=-\left(x^2-1\right)+1$

Question 214

Converting the polar equation $2r\sin(\theta)=r^2-1$ into cartesian form gives the equation

A. $y^2=(1-x)^2$ **B.** $x^2+(y-1)^2=2$ **C.** $y^2+(x-1)^2=2$

D. $y-1=2(x-1)$ **E.** $y^2=2\left(x^2+1\right)$

Question 215

Converting the cartesian equation $2x^2+2y^2=32$, into polar form gives the equation

A. $r=4$ **B.** $r=16$ **C.** $(r-1)^2+\sin^2(\theta)=1$

D. $(r-1)=2(\sin(\theta)-1)$ **E.** $r=\pm\sin(\theta)$

Question 216

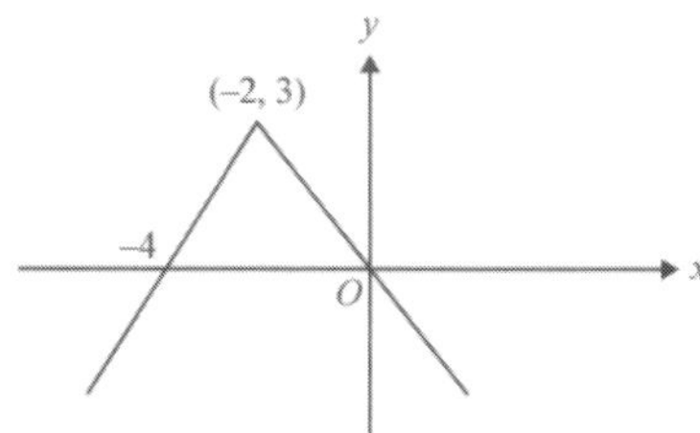

The rule of the function whose graph is shown above is

A. $y=-\frac{3}{2}|x|+3$ **B.** $y=\frac{2}{3}|x+3|+2$ **C.** $y=\frac{2}{3}|2+x|+3$

D. $y=-\frac{3}{2}|2-x|+3$ **E.** $y=-\frac{3}{2}|x+2|+3$

[VCAA 2014 MM]

Question 217

The rule of the relation determined by the parametric equations $x = 2\operatorname{cosec}(t)+1$ and $y = 3\cot(t)-1$ is

A. $\frac{(x-1)^2}{4}-\frac{(y+1)^2}{9}=1$

B. $\frac{(y+1)^2}{9}-\frac{(x-1)^2}{4}=1$

C. $\frac{(x-1)^2}{4}+\frac{(y+1)^2}{9}=1$

D. $\frac{(y+1)^2}{3}-\frac{(x-1)^2}{2}=1$

E. $\frac{(x-1)^2}{2}-\frac{(y+1)^2}{3}=1$

[VCAA 2013 SM]

Question 218

The ellipse $\frac{(x-2)^2}{9}+\frac{(y-3)^2}{4}=1$ can be expressed in parametric form as

A. $x = 2+3t$ and $y = 3+2\sqrt{1+t^2}$

B. $x = 2+3\sec(t)$ and $y = 3+2\tan(t)$

C. $x = 2+9\cos(t)$ and $y = 3+4\sin(t)$

D. $x = 3+2\cos(t)$ and $y = 2+3\sin(t)$

E. $x = 2+3\cos(t)$ and $y = 3+2\sin(t)$

[VCAA 2015 SM]

Question 219

Plot the following points on the polar coordinate axes shown here.

$A\left[1,\frac{\pi}{4}\right]$ $B\left[-2,\frac{\pi}{4}\right]$ $C\left[3,\frac{3\pi}{4}\right]$ $D\left[2,-\frac{5\pi}{4}\right]$

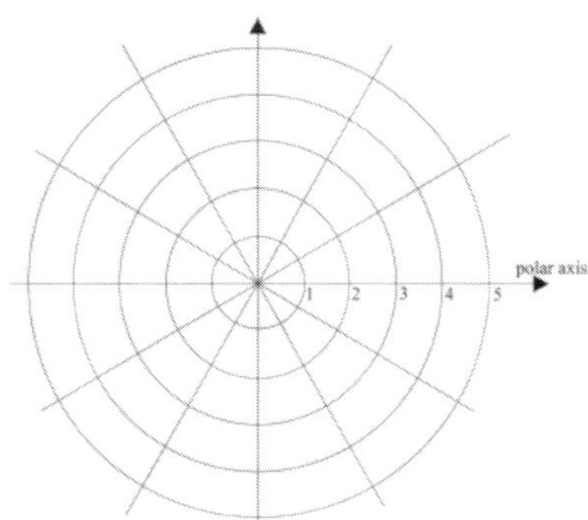

Question 220

Consider the polar equation $r = \dfrac{1}{1-\sin(\theta)}$ for $0 \le \theta \le 2\pi$.

a. Complete this table, using values correct to 2 decimal places where necessary.

θ	0	$\frac{\pi}{6}$	$\frac{\pi}{3}$	$\frac{\pi}{2}$	$\frac{2\pi}{3}$	π	$\frac{4\pi}{3}$	$\frac{3\pi}{2}$	$\frac{5\pi}{3}$	2π
r										

b. Hence sketch the graph of $r = \dfrac{1}{1-\sin(\theta)}$ for $0 \le \theta \le 2\pi$ on the axes shown here.

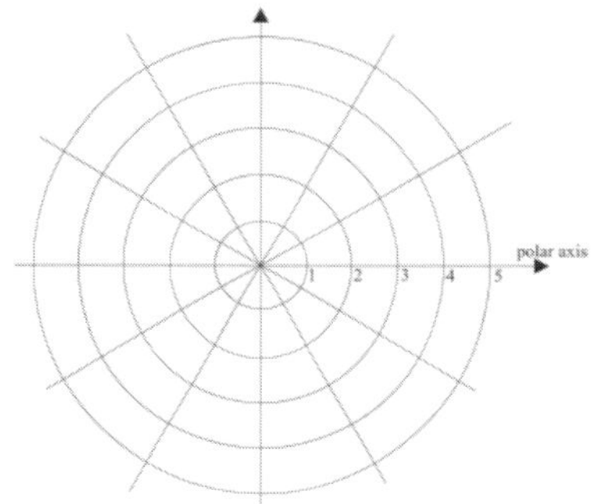

Question 221

Sketch the graph with equation $y^2 = 4(x+4)$ showing the coordinates of the vertex and any axis intercepts.

Question 222

Consider the ellipse with equation $\dfrac{(x-2)^2}{4} + (y+1)^2 = 1$.

Find the coordinates of the points of intersection of this ellipse and the line with equation $y = x - 2$.

Question 223

A curve C has parametric equations $x = \sqrt{t-2}$ and $y = 2t$, for $2 \le t \le 6$.

a. Find the cartesian equation of C.

b. Sketch the curve on the axes provided.

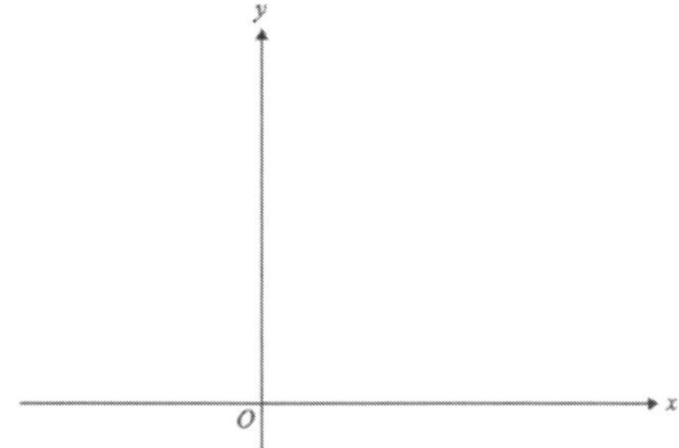

Question 224

Express $\frac{3x}{(2-x)(4+x^2)}$ in partial fractions.

Question 225

Let $f(x)=\sec(4x)$.

Sketch the graph of f for $x\in\left[-\frac{\pi}{4},\frac{\pi}{4}\right]$. Label any asymptotes with their equations and label any turning points and the endpoints with their coordinates.

[VCAA 2022 SM]

Solutions: A1

Question 1 E

$6^{\frac{1}{2}} = \sqrt{6}$ is irrational (similar to $\sqrt{2}$).

(The other alternatives are all rational:

$3.14159 = \dfrac{314159}{100000}$, $0.\dot{9} = 1$, $\sqrt[3]{64} = 4$ and $\dfrac{\sqrt{3}}{\sqrt{12}} = \dfrac{\sqrt{3}}{2\sqrt{3}} = \dfrac{1}{2}$.)

Question 2 B

As two of the factors must be even, the expression is divisible by 4; as any three consecutive integers must contain one that is a multiple of 3, the expression is divisible by 3.

So $n(n+1)(n+2)(n+3)$ is divisible by 12.

(A simple counterexample shows the other alternatives are false: if $n = 1$, the given expression is equal to 24 and this is not divisible by any of 11, 13, 14 or 15.)

Question 3 E

Since $(\sqrt{2}+1)(\sqrt{2}-1) = (\sqrt{2})^2 - 1 = 2 - 1 = 1$, multiplying the denominator by $\sqrt{2}-1$ will rationalise it.

However, if the expression is not to change its value, you can only multiply it by 1, which can be written as $\dfrac{\sqrt{2}-1}{\sqrt{2}-1}$.

(Alternatives **A**–**C** will change the value of the expression; alternative **D** gives a denominator of $(\sqrt{2}+1)^2 = 3+2\sqrt{2}$, which is not rational.)

Question 4 C

n is one of 4, 9, 16, …, so $n-1$ is one of 3, 8, 15, …, none of which is a perfect square.

(If $n = 4$, $\sqrt{n}-1 = 1$ and $2\sqrt{n} = 4$, both perfect squares; $n^2 - 2n + 1 = (n-1)^2$, a perfect square; $n^2 - 2\sqrt{n} + 1 = (\sqrt{n}-1)^2$, also a perfect square since n is a perfect square.)

Question 5

a. $A \cup B$ is the set of all elements that are members of set A or set B (or both).

So $A \cup B = \{1, 2, 3, 4, 5, 7\}$.

b. $A \cap C$ is the set of all elements that are members of set A and set B.

So $A \cap C = \{7\}$.

c. $B \cup C = \{1, 2, 3, 4, 6, 7, 8\}$

So $A \cap (B \cup C) = \{1, 3, 7\}$.

d. $A \cap B = \{1, 3\}$, $A \cap C = \{7\}$

So $(A \cap B) \cup (A \cap C) = \{1, 3, 7\}$.

In general, $A \cap (B \cup C) = (A \cap B) \cup (A \cap C)$.

Intersection is distributive over union.

e. $A \cup B = \{1, 2, 3, 4, 5, 7\}$

$(A \cup B)'$ is the set of elements not in $A \cup B$.

So $(A \cup B)' = \{6, 8, 9\}$.

f. $A' = \{2, 4, 6, 8, 9\}$, $B' = \{5, 6, 7, 8, 9\}$

So $A' \cap B' = \{6, 8, 9\}$.

In general, $(A \cup B)' = A' \cap B'$.

Question 6

a. The set $A = \{2, 4, 6\}$ has 8 subsets.

The power set, $P(A)$ is the following:

the empty set: $\varnothing$

subsets of size 1: $\{2\}$, $\{4\}$, $\{6\}$

subsets of size 2: $\{2,4\}$, $\{2,6\}$, $\{4,6\}$

subsets of size 3: $\{2, 4, 6\}$

b. For every subset of A, there are two possibilities for each element $x \in A$.

Either x will be in the subset, or it will not.

Therefore, for all m there will be 2^m different choices in making a subset of A.

Therefore, the number of subsets of A is 2^m.

Question 7

a. $\sqrt{197} = 14.0$, correct to one decimal place.

b. Check for divisibility by primes less than 14.

197 is prime as 2, 3, 5, 7, 11 and 13 are not factors.

Question 8

a. The primes which divide 40! are the primes in the list $\{1, 2, 3, ..., 48, 49, 50\}$.

These are $\{2, 3, 5, 7, 11, 13, 17, 19, 23, 29, 31, 37\}$.

b. A zero at the end of 40! occurs when we have a product 2×5.

We only need to count the factors of 5 in 40!.

One each for $5, 10, 15, 20$.

Two for 25.

One each for $30, 35, 40$.

So $4+2+3=9$.

Hence 40! ends in 9 zeros.

Question 9

Suppose there are finitely many prime numbers $p_1, p_2, ..., p_k$.

This means that every integer greater than 1 is either equal to one of the p_i values or it is divisible by at least one of them.

Consider the number $N = p_1 p_2 ... p_k + 1$.

Clearly $N \neq p_i$, as it is larger than all of them.

Also, N gives remainder 1 when divided by each p_i, so it is not divisible by any of them.

However, this situation is impossible.

Hence our assumption that there are finitely many primes was incorrect, and so there are infinitely many prime numbers.

Question 10

$0.\dot{2}\dot{7} = 0.272727...$ (1)

Multiply both sides by 10^2:

$0.\dot{2}\dot{7} \times 10^2 = 27.272727...$ (2)

Subtract (1) from (2):

$$0.\dot{2}\dot{7} \times \left(10^2 - 1\right) = 27$$

$$\begin{aligned} 0.\dot{2}\dot{7} &= \frac{27}{10^2 - 1} \\ &= \frac{27}{99} \\ &= \frac{3}{11} \end{aligned}$$

Question 11

a. Either n is even or $(n-1)$ is even, so $n^2 - n = n(n-1)$ is even (the product of an even and an odd number).

Adding 41 to an even number gives an odd number.

So $n^2 - n + 41$ is odd.

b. The key to finding a composite number is to look at the constant term, 41.

Substituting $n = 41$ will have 41 as a factor.

In fact, $41^2 - 41 + 41 = 41^2$, which is not prime.

Question 12

Suppose that $\log_2(3)$ is rational and prove that this gives a contradiction.

$\log_2(3) = \frac{p}{q}$ where p and q are integers with no common factors.

Then by the definition of a logarithm:

$$3 = 2^{\frac{p}{q}} \Rightarrow 3^q = 2^p$$

But the left side is odd and the right side is even, a contradiction.

Hence $\log_2(3)$ is an irrational number.

Question 13

Suppose there exists $m, n \in Z^+$ such that $m^2 - n^2 = 1$.

$$(m+n)(m-n) = 1$$

Case 1:

$m + n = 1$ and $m - n = 1$

So $m = 1$, $n = 0$.

Case 2:

$m + n = -1$ and $m - n = -1$

So $m = -1$, $n = 0$.

As $m, n \in Z^+$, both cases provide a contradiction.

Hence no positive integers m and n exist such that $m^2 - n^2 = 1$.

Question 14

a. The contrapositive is:
If n is odd then n^2 is odd.

Let $n = 2k + 1$, then n is odd and

$$\begin{aligned} n^2 &= (2k+1)^2 \\ &= 4k^2 + 4k + 1 \\ &= 2\left(2k^2 + 2k\right) + 1 \end{aligned}$$

$2\left(2k^2 + 2k\right) + 1$ is 1 more than a multiple of 2 and is thus odd.

Hence, by the contrapositive, if n^2 is even then n is even.

b. The contrapositive is:

If x is even, then x^2-6x+5 is odd.

Let $x=2k$ for $k\in Z$.

$$\begin{aligned}x^2-6x+5&=(2k)^2-6(2k)+5\\&=4k^2-12k+5\\&=4k^2-12k+4+1\\&=2\left(2k^2-6k+2\right)+1\end{aligned}$$

So $x^2-6x+5=2a+1$ where a is the integer $2k^2-6k+2$.

Thus x^2-6x+5 is odd.

Hence, by the contrapositive, if x^2-6x+5 is even then x is odd.

Question 15

Suppose $x\le y$.

Subtracting y from both sides gives $x-y\le 0$.

$$\sqrt{x^2}-\sqrt{y^2}\le 0$$
$$\left(\sqrt{x}-\sqrt{y}\right)\left(\sqrt{x}+\sqrt{y}\right)\le 0$$

Dividing both sides by $\sqrt{x}+\sqrt{y}$ (which is positive) gives $\sqrt{x}-\sqrt{y}\le 0$.

Adding $\sqrt{y}$ to both sides gives $\sqrt{x}\le\sqrt{y}$.

Question 16

a. Required to prove that if $x<y$, then $x<\frac{x+y}{2}$.

$$\begin{aligned}x<y&\Rightarrow\frac{x}{2}<\frac{y}{2}\\&\Rightarrow\frac{x}{2}+\frac{x}{2}<\frac{x}{2}+\frac{y}{2}\\&\Rightarrow x<\frac{x+y}{2}\end{aligned}$$

b. Suppose that $0.\dot{9}<1$.

Using the result, $x<y\Rightarrow x<\frac{x+y}{2}$ gives:

$$\begin{aligned}0.\dot{9}&<\frac{0.\dot{9}+1}{2}\\&<\frac{1.\dot{9}}{2}\\&<0.\dot{9}\end{aligned}$$

$0.\dot{9}<0.\dot{9}$ is a contradiction and so $0.\dot{9}<1$ is not true.

Hence $0.\dot{9}\ge 1$ is true.

However, since $0.\dot{9}\not>1$, then $0.\dot{9}=1$.

Question 17

Integers greater than 5, can be expressed in one of the following forms:

$6n$, $6n+1$, $6n+2$, $6n+3$, $6n+4$, $6n+5$

Any prime $p\ge 5$ can only have the form $6n+1$ or $6n+5$ (the other forms are composite).

Case 1:

$$\begin{aligned}p^2-1&=(6n+1)^2-1\\&=36n^2+12n\\&=12\left(3n^2+n\right)\text{ where }3n^2+n\in Z^+\end{aligned}$$

Case 2:

$$\begin{aligned}p^2-1&=(6n+5)^2-1\\&=36n^2+60n+24\\&=12\left(3n^2+5n+2\right)\text{ where }3n^2+5n+2\in Z^+\end{aligned}$$

Hence p^2-1 is divisible by 12.

Question 18

Consider $n=1$: $5\times 7^1+1=36$ and 36 is divisible by 6.

So true for $n=1$.

Assume true for $n=k$, that is, $5\times 7^k+1=6m$ where $m\in Z^+$.

Now consider $n=k+1$, that is, $5\times 7^{k+1}+1$.

From the assumption, $5\times 7^k=6m-1$, and substituting we obtain:

$$\begin{aligned}5\times 7^{k+1}+1&=7(6m-1)+1\\&=6(7m-1)\end{aligned}$$

This is divisible by 6, so if true for $n=k$ then true for $n=k+1$, and since true for $n=1$, $5\times 7^n+1$ is divisible by 6 $\forall n\in Z^+$.

Question 19

Consider $n=1$: $\text{LHS}=2\times 2^0=1\times 2=2=\text{RHS}$

So true for $n=1$.

Assume true for $n=k$, that is, $\sum_{r=1}^{k}(r+1)2^{r-1}=k2^k$ where $k\in Z^+$.

Now consider $n=k+1$:

$$\sum_{r=1}^{k+1}(r+1)2^{r-1}=k2^k+(k+1+1)2^{k+1-1}$$

$$\begin{aligned}&=2^k(k+k+2)\\&=2(k+1)2^k\\&=(k+1)2^{k+1}\end{aligned}$$

So if true for $n=k$ then true for $n=k+1$, and since true for $n=1$, therefore

$\sum_{r=1}^{n}(r+1)2^{r-1}=n2^{n}$ is true $\forall n\in Z^{+}$.

Question 20

Consider $n=10$:

$\text{LHS}=2^{10}=1024$ and $\text{RHS}=10^{3}=1000$

So true for $n=10$.

Assume true for $n=k$, that is, $2^{k}>k^{3}$ where $k\in Z^{+},k\geq 10$.

Now consider $n=k+1$, that is, $2^{k+1}>(k+1)^{3}$.

Consider $\text{LHS}-\text{RHS}>0$ where

$$\begin{aligned}\text{LHS}-\text{RHS}&=2^{k+1}-(k+1)^{3}\\&=2\times 2^{k}-(k^{3}+3k^{2}+3k+1)\end{aligned}$$

$$\begin{aligned}\text{LHS}-\text{RHS}&>2k^{3}-(k^{3}+3k^{2}+3k+1)\\&=k^{3}-(3k^{2}+3k+1)\\&>k^{3}-(3k^{2}+3k^{2}+3k^{2})\quad(\text{since } k>1)\\&=k^{2}(k-9)\\&>0\quad(\text{since } k\geq 10)\end{aligned}$$

So if true for $n=k$ then true for $n=k+1$, and since true for $n=1$, $2^{n}>n^{3}$ for $\forall n\in Z^{+},n\geq 10$.

Solutions: A2

Question 21 E

The maximum number of edges at any vertex is 7 since the graph is simple.

As there are 8 vertices, the total number of edges is at most $\frac{1}{2}(7\times 8)=28$ (each edge joins two vertices so divide by 2 to avoid double counting).

Question 22 B

For a tree with n vertices the number of edges is $n-1$.

For a tree with 5 vertices the number of edges is $5-1=4$.

Question 23 E

For a planar graph $v-e+f=2$.

If a graph has 5 faces:

$$v-e+5=2$$
$$v-e=2-5$$
$$v-e=-3$$
$$e-v=3$$

The graph must have 3 more edges than vertices.

A planar graph with five vertices and eight edges meets this requirement.

Question 24 D

PTQSR is not a path for the graph since there is no edge connecting the vertices *S* and *R*.

Question 25 D

A graph is planar if it can be drawn without any edges that cross.

The graph in **E** is a planar graph without any redrawing.

The graph in **A** can be redrawn so that no edges cross.

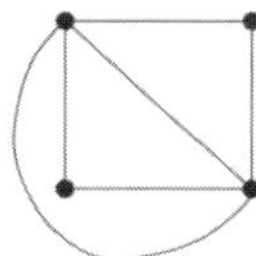

The graph in **B** can be redrawn so that no edges cross.

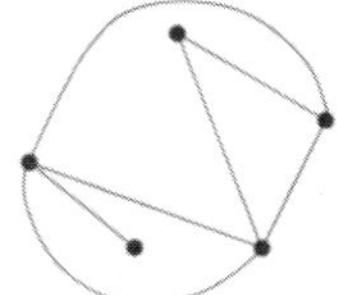

The graph in **C** can be redrawn so that no edges cross.

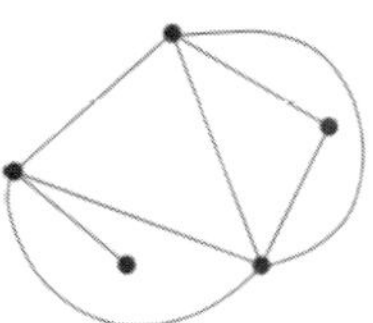

It is not possible to redraw the graph in **D** so that no edges cross.

Alternatively, the graph in alternative **D** is the complete graph on 5 vertices and this is known to be non-planar.

Question 26 E

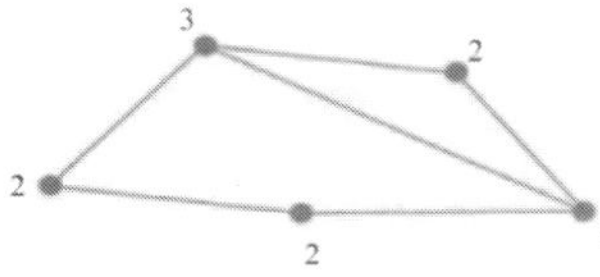

The vertices have degrees 2, 3, 2, 3 and 2.

The sum of the degrees is $3\times 2+2\times 3=12$.

Question 27 C

For an Eulerian circuit to be possible then all of the vertices in the graph must have even degree.

Four vertices in this graph have odd degree.

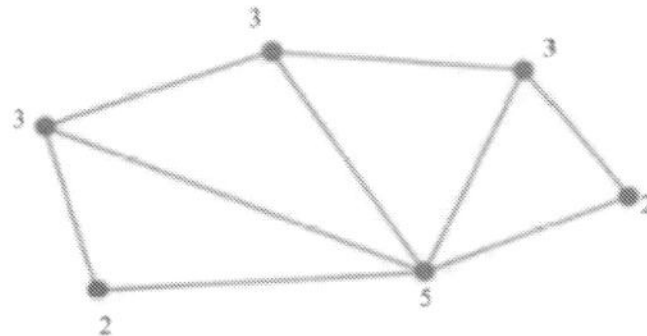

The minimum number of edges that must be added is 2.

An edge joining one pair of vertices with odd degree and an edge joining the other pair of vertices with odd degree.

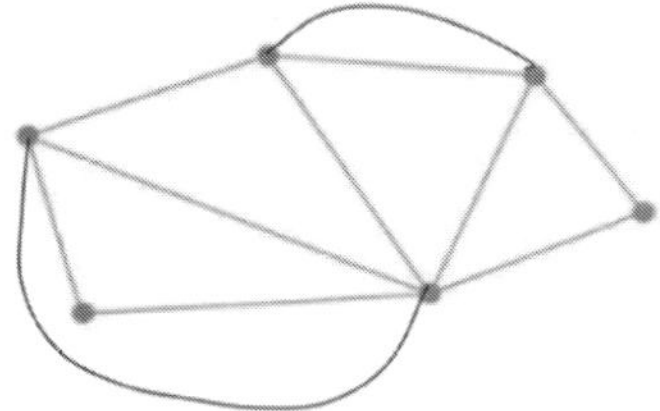

Question 28 A

For two graphs to be isomorphic they must be exactly the same.

Graph 1 has 4 vertices and Graph 2 has 5 vertices so they cannot be isomorphic.

Question 29 A

To complete the adjacency matrix, firstly start at *P*.

There is one road loop connecting town *P* to itself.

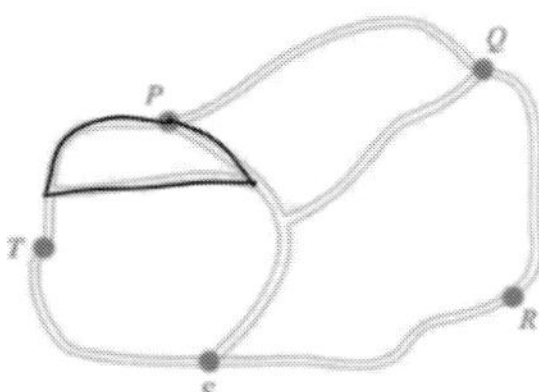

This gives the following information for the adjacency matrix.

$$\begin{array}{c} \\ P \\ Q \\ R \\ S \\ T \end{array}\begin{array}{c} \begin{array}{ccccc} P & Q & R & S & T \end{array} \\ \begin{bmatrix} 1 & & & & \\ & & & & \\ & & & & \\ & & & & \\ 2 & 1 & 0 & 2 & 0 \end{bmatrix} \end{array}$$

There are three possible routes from *P* to *Q* which do not involve passing through other towns.

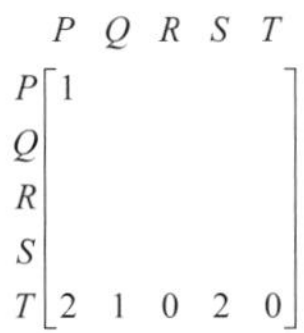

The adjacency matrix becomes

$$\begin{array}{c} \\ P \\ Q \\ R \\ S \\ T \end{array}\begin{array}{c} \begin{array}{ccccc} P & Q & R & S & T \end{array} \\ \begin{bmatrix} 1 & 3 & & & \\ 3 & & & & \\ & & & & \\ & & & & \\ 2 & 1 & 0 & 2 & 0 \end{bmatrix} \end{array}$$

At this point the matrices in **B**, **C**, **D** and **E** can be eliminated as possibilities.

Question 30 D

$$\begin{aligned} v+f-e&=2 \\ 7+f-9&=2 \\ f&=4 \end{aligned}$$

Question 31 D

A Hamiltonian cycle starts and ends at the same vertex and passes through every vertex exactly once.

There is no edge from *E* to *D*, so *DCBAGFED* is not a Hamiltonian cycle for this graph.

Question 32 B

There is no edge connecting vertices 3 and 5.

The tree shown here cannot be a spanning tree, since it has an edge connecting vertices 3 and 5.

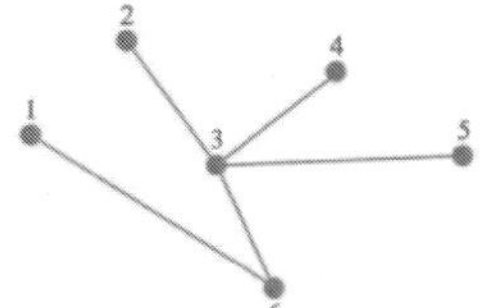

Question 33 C

A graph that could be used to display this information is a bipartite graph as shown below.

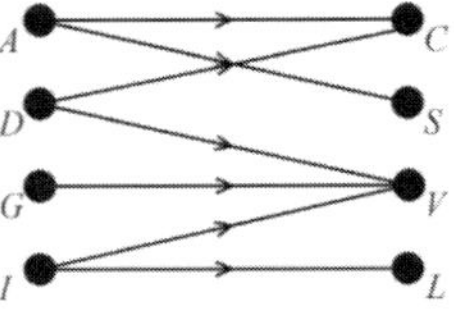

A bipartite graph is neither connected nor a tree, but it is planar as it can be redrawn without any edges crossing.

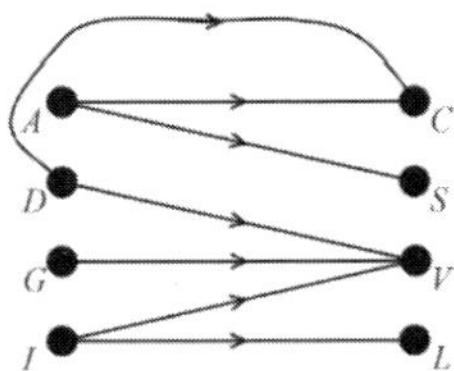

Only two of the four statements are true.

Question 34 E

$$\begin{array}{c} \\ J \\ K \\ L \\ M \end{array}\begin{array}{c} \begin{array}{cccc} J & K & L & M \end{array} \\ \begin{bmatrix} 1 & 3 & 0 & 2 \\ 3 & 0 & 1 & 2 \\ 0 & 1 & 0 & 2 \\ 2 & 2 & 2 & 0 \end{bmatrix} \end{array}$$

From this adjacency matrix, there is/are:

One connection between *J* and itself.

Three connections between *J* and *K*.

Two connections between *J* and *M*.

One connection between *K* and *L*.

Two connections between *K* and *M*.

Two connections between *L* and *M*.

The only one of the graph networks that could be represented using this adjacency matrix is shown below.

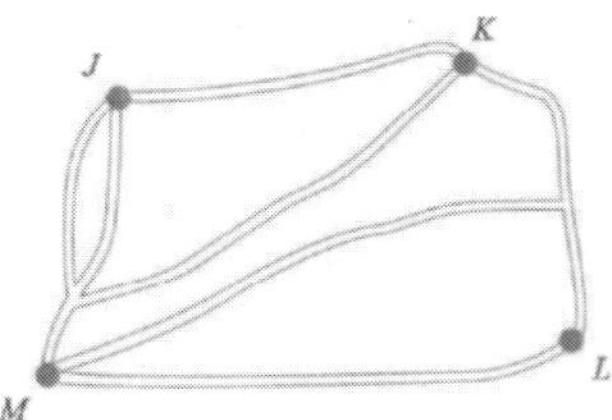

Question 35

a. 7 edges (one less than the number of vertices).

b. The sum of the degrees is $2\times 7=14$.

The two vertices given have degree sum 7, so that leaves a degree sum of 7 for the remaining six vertices.

So five of the remaining vertices must have degree 1 and one must have degree 2.

Three trees can be drawn in this case.

- The degree 4 and degree 3 vertices are directly connected and the degree 2 vertex connects to the degree 3 vertex.
- The degree 4 and degree 3 vertices are directly connected and the degree 2 vertex connects to the degree 4 vertex.
- The degree 4 and degree 3 vertices are not directly connected (each has the degree 2 vertex as intermediary).

Question 36

a. A circuit starts and finishes at the same vertex.

ABCDEA is a Hamiltonian circuit (each vertex is passed through once except for the start/end vertex).

Vertices *B* and *C* are of odd degree, so no circuit exists that passes over each edge exactly once, i.e. there is no Eulerian circuit.

b. An Eulerian path exists, starting at *B* (or *C*) and ending at *C* (or *B*).

This is equivalent to saying that the graph is traversable: you can draw it as described by the Eulerian path.

c. *AE* and *DE* cannot be removed, since they would lead to four vertices of odd degree, i.e. an Eulerian path would exist.

d. For an Eulerian circuit, all vertices must be of even degree.

So edge *BC* must be removed.

e. The only possibilities for a new edge are from joining *A* to *C*, to *A* or *D* or *B* to *D* since the resulting graph is to be simple.

Joining *A* to *D* will not do because it will create two extra vertices of odd degree.

Either of the other possibilities works (an odd degree becomes even and an even degree becomes odd).

f. *G* is drawn with no edges crossing, so it is planar.

For *G*, the values are $v=5$, $f=4$ and $e=7$.

Then $v+f-e=5+4-7=2$.

Question 37

a. A simple connected graph *G* with *v* vertices can be constructed by joining one vertex to each of the other $(v-1)$ vertices.

So the minimum number of edges that *G* can have is $(v-1)$.

b. The number of edges in K_n is $\dfrac{n(n-1)}{2}$.

c. The complement of K_n is a graph with no edges.

d. The number of edges in H' is $\dfrac{n(n-1)}{2}-e$.

e. From parts a. and b., $e\geq n-1$ and $e\leq\dfrac{n(n-1)}{2}$.

So $n-1\leq e\leq\dfrac{n^2-n}{2}$ and hence $2n-2\leq 2e\leq n^2-n$.

Question 38

K_n has $\dfrac{n(n-1)}{2}$ edges and K_{n-1} has $\dfrac{(n-1)(n-2)}{2}$ edges.

In a graph *G* with *n* vertices, any subgraph with $(n-1)$ vertices has at most $\frac{1}{2}(n-1)(n-2)$ edges.

Hence if *G* has more than $\frac{1}{2}(n-1)(n-2)$ edges, the *n*th vertex must be connected by an edge to the subgraph containing the remaining vertices.

Question 39

A simple graph is bipartite if and only if each of its circuits is of even length.

If *G* has an odd number of vertices, it cannot contain a circuit visiting every vertex.

Hence *G* is not Hamiltonian.

Question 40

a. Suppose that $K_{3,3}$ is planar (proof by contradiction).

$K_{3,3}$ has 6 vertices and 9 edges.

Using $v+f=e+2$:

$6+f=9+2$ and so $f=5$ i.e. $K_{3,3}$ has 5 faces.

$K_{3,3}$ is bipartite and hence none of the faces in its plane representation are triangular.

Hence each face has at least 4 edges.

Counting the edges around all 5 faces, there are at least $4\times 5=20$ edges.

Since every edge is on the border of two faces, each edge has been counted twice.

So $K_{3,3}$ has at least $\dfrac{20}{2}=10$ edges.

This is a contradiction, since $K_{3,3}$ has only 9 edges.

Hence $K_{3,3}$ is not planar.

b. Since every face is bounded by at least 3 edges the result follows by counting the edges around each face.

Every edge bounds (at most) 2 faces and so $2e \geq 3f$.

Using $2e \geq 3f$ and $v+f=e+2$.

$$
\begin{aligned}
2e &\geq 3f \\
2e &\geq 3(e+2-v) \\
2e &\geq 3e+6-3v \\
e &\leq 3v-6
\end{aligned}
$$

c. For K_5, $v=5$ and $e=\dfrac{5\times 4}{2}=10$.

Using $e \leq 3v-6$ gives $10 \leq 9$ $(3\times 5-6)$ which is false and so K_5 is not planar.

d. H has $v \geq 11$ vertices and e edges.

H' has $\dfrac{v(v-1)}{2}-e$ edges.

As $e \leq 3v-6$, then $\dfrac{v(v-1)}{2}-e \leq 3v-6$.

$$
\begin{aligned}
e &\geq \frac{v(v-1)}{2}-3v+6 \\
3v-6 &\geq \frac{v(v-1)}{2}-3v+6 \\
6v-12 &\geq v^2-v-6v+12 \\
v^2-13v+24 &\leq 0
\end{aligned}
$$

Solving for v gives $2.22... \leq v \leq 10.77...$.

For $v \geq 11$, $v^2-13v+24>0$ and so H and H' cannot both be planar.

Solutions: A3

Question 41 D

$(A+B)' = A' \cdot B'$ so **D** is incorrect.

Question 42 D

The middle shaded region is $R \cap S \cap T$.

The outer shaded region is $R' \cap S' \cap T'$.

Thus the shaded regions are the union of $R \cap S \cap T$ and $R' \cap S' \cap T'$, i.e. $(R \cap S \cap T) \cup (R' \cap S' \cap T')$.

Question 43 B

If both x and y are zero then the 'and' gate has an input of 0, 1 and will have an output of 0 so the answer is **A** or **B**.

If x is 0 and y is 1 then the 'and' gate has an input of 0, 0 and will have an output of 0.

So **B** is correct (check other inputs work.)

Question 44 B

$$\begin{aligned}(x' \cdot (y+z))' &= (x')' + (y+z)' \\ &= x + y' \cdot z'\end{aligned}$$

Question 45 E

Rewrite $\sim(p \vee q)$ as a boolean expression, i.e. $(p+q)'$.

$$(p+q)' = p' \cdot q'$$

Then $p' \cdot q'$ can be written as $\sim p \wedge \sim q$ using propositional logic notation.

Question 46 E

$$\begin{aligned}[(X \cup Y') \cap Z]' &= (X \cup Y')' \cup Z' \\ &= (X' \cup Y'') \cup Z' \\ &= (X' \cap Y) \cup Z'\end{aligned}$$

Question 47 B

By inspection, the only time that Z is 0 is when X and Y are both 1.

So the correct expression is $(X \cap Y)'$.

Question 48 C

Looking at the 1s in the Karnaugh map gives the boolean expression $x' \cdot y' + x \cdot y' + x' \cdot y$.

This simplifies as follows:

$$\begin{aligned}x' \cdot y' + x \cdot y' + x' \cdot y &= x' \cdot (y' + y) + x \cdot y' \\ &= x' + x \cdot y'\end{aligned}$$

Question 49 B

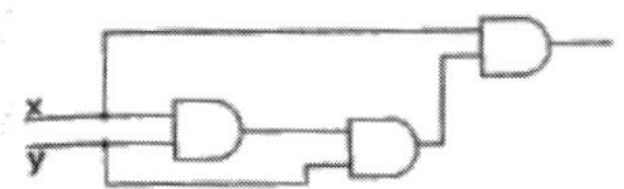

This circuit can be written as a boolean algebra expression $x \cdot ((x \cdot y) \cdot y)$.

This can be simplified as follows:

$$\begin{aligned}x \cdot ((x \cdot y) \cdot y) &= x \cdot x \cdot y \cdot y \\ &= x \cdot y\end{aligned}$$

This is x and y and therefore the simplified circuit is

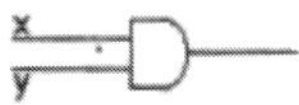

Question 50 C

Check each alternative in turn:

A. not p does not imply p

B. not p and p cannot be true together

C. either not p is true or p is true; so this is a tautology!

D. equivalent to p

E. equivalent to p

Question 51 A

The boolean expression for this circuit is

$$\begin{aligned}(x' \cdot y) \cdot (y' + z) \cdot z' &= (x' \cdot y) \cdot (y' \cdot z' + z \cdot z') \\ &= (x' \cdot y) \cdot (y' \cdot z' + 0) \\ &= (x' \cdot y) \cdot (y' \cdot z') \\ &= x' \cdot (y \cdot y') \cdot z' \\ &= x' \cdot 0 \cdot z' \\ &= 0\end{aligned}$$

Question 52 D

$y \rightarrow x$ is taken to be false when y is true and x is false, otherwise it is true:

y	x	$y \rightarrow x$
T	T	T
T	F	F
F	T	T
F	F	T

So the correct truth table is in **D**.

Question 53 D

Perform a desk check.

The sequence of values produced (starting with 1) is 1, 4, 13, 40, 121.

The output is 121 as the algorithm performs the calculation $3 \times 40 + 1 = 121$ where $40 < 50$.

Question 54

$$\begin{aligned} y' + x' \cdot z + (x \cdot y)' &= y' + x' \cdot z + x' + y' \\ &= y' + x' \cdot z + x' \\ &= y' + x' \\ &= (x \cdot y)' \end{aligned}$$

Question 55

a.

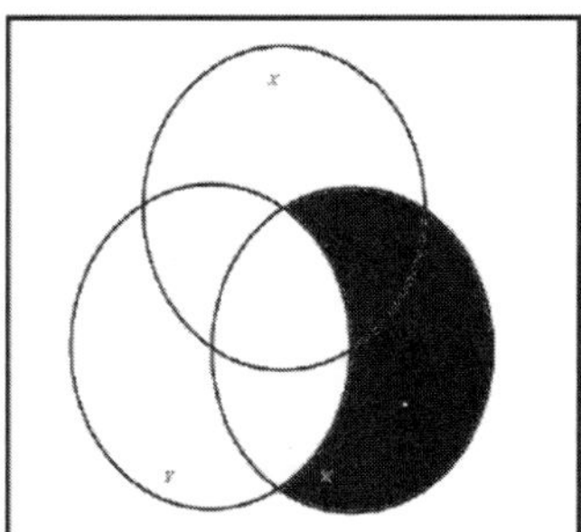

b. The region shaded in the diagram in simplest form is $Y' \cap Z$.

Question 56

$(x+y) \cdot (x \cdot y)'$ can be read as:

(x or y) and not (x and y)

The following circuit is equivalent to this expression.

Question 57

a. $z = (x \wedge y) \vee (\sim x \vee \sim y)$.

b.

x	y	z
T	T	T
T	F	T
F	T	T
F	F	T

c. The expression is a tautology since it is always true (T) regardless of what the input values of x and y are.

d. Required to show that $x \cdot y + (x' + y') = 1$.

$$\begin{aligned} x \cdot y + (x' + y') &= (x' + y') + x \cdot y \\ &= (x' + y' + x) \cdot (x' + y' + y) \\ &= (1 + y') \cdot (1 + x') \\ &= 1 \cdot 1 \\ &= 1 \end{aligned}$$

Question 58

A	B	$A \vee B$ A or B	$A \wedge B$ A and B	$\sim(A \wedge B)$	$(A \vee B) \wedge \sim(A \wedge B)$ (A or B) and not(A or B)
T	T	T	T	F	F
T	F	T	F	T	T
F	T	T	F	T	T
F	F	F	F	T	F

Question 59

a.

n	1900	1948	1995	2000
p	T	T	F	T
q	T	F	F	T
s	F	F	F	T

b. n is not divisible by 400.

c. n is divisible by 100 and not divisible by 400.

d. If n is divisible by 400 then n is also divisible by 4.

e.

n	1900	1948	1995	2000
$\sim s$	T	T	T	F
$q \wedge \sim s$	T	F	F	F
$p \wedge \sim(q \wedge \sim s)$	F	T	F	T
$s \to p$	T	T	T	T

f. Required to show that $p \cdot (q \cdot s')' = p \cdot q' + p \cdot s$.

$$\begin{aligned} \text{LHS} &= p \cdot (q \cdot s')' \\ &= p \cdot (q' + s) \\ &= p \cdot q' + p \cdot s \\ &= \text{RHS} \end{aligned}$$

Question 60

a.

		x	
		0	1
y	0	1	1
	1	1	0

b. From the Karnaugh map you can see that $z = 1$ if $x = 0$ or $y = 0$, so the expression can be simplified to $z = x' + y'$.

Question 61

Use repeated division by 2 and record the remainders in reverse.

This is shown in the following table.

Division	Quotient	Remainder
$347 \div 2$	173	1
$173 \div 2$	86	1
$86 \div 2$	43	0
$43 \div 2$	21	1
$21 \div 2$	10	1
$10 \div 2$	5	0
$5 \div 2$	2	1
$2 \div 2$	1	0
$1 \div 2$	0	1

So $347_{10} = 101011011_2$.

Question 62

If a and b are integers with $b > 0$, then there are unique integers q (quotient) and r (remainder) such that $a = qb + r$ where $0 \le r < b$.

We apply the algorithm as follows:

$$\begin{aligned}315 &= 5\times 56+35\\ 56 &= 1\times 35+21\\ 35 &= 1\times 21+14\\ 21 &= 1\times 14+7\\ 14 &= 2\times 7+0\end{aligned}$$

Hence $\text{HCF}(56, 315) = 7$.

Question 63

a. Here we rewrite $P(x)$ by successively factoring out x as follows:

$$\begin{aligned}P(x) &= (2x^2 - 7x + 4)x - 5\\ &= ((2x-7)x+4)x-5\end{aligned}$$

b. Evaluate $P(5)$.

$$\begin{aligned}P(5) &= ((2\times 5-7)\times 5+4)\times 5-5\\ &= (3\times 5+4)\times 5-5\\ &= 19\times 5-5\\ &= 95-5\\ &= 90\end{aligned}$$

c. Evaluate $P(5)$ directly and count the number of multiplications and additions.

$$\begin{aligned}P(5) &= (2\times 5\times 5\times 5)-(7\times 5\times 5)+(4\times 5)-5\\ &= 250-175+20-5\\ &= 90\end{aligned}$$

There are $3+2+1=6$ multiplications and 3 additions.

Evaluating $P(5)$ by Horner's method requires 3 multiplications and 3 additions.

Hence Horner's method is more efficient than direct evaluation.

Question 64

```
count ← 0
remainder ← 470
while remainder ≥ 9
    count ← count + 1
    remainder ← remainder − 9
end while
print count, remainder
```

Question 65

a. Let t represent the current term of the sequence and use n to track the number of iterations.

```
n ← 1
t ← 2
while t ≤ 2000
    n ← n + 1
    t ← 4t + 1
end while
print n
```

b. The table below shows the desk check.

n	t
1	2
2	9
3	37
4	149
5	597
6	2389

The output is 6 i.e., the smallest value of n for which $t_n > 2000$ is 6.

Solutions: A4

Question 66 D

For an arithmetic sequence, we require a common difference between any two consecutive terms.

The sequence in alternative **A** is geometric with common ratio $r = 2$.

The sequence in alternative **B** has a difference between consecutive terms that forms a geometric sequence i.e. the difference between any two consecutive terms is doubling (not constant).

The sequences in alternatives **C** and **E** do not have a common difference.

The sequence in alternative **D** shows the first five terms of an arithmetic sequence with $a = -7$ and $d = 4$.

Question 67 C

As $t_4 < t_2$, we know that $d < 0$.

Using $2d = t_4 - t_2$ gives $2d = 32 - 46 = -14$.

So $d = -7$.

$t_2 = 46$ and so $a + (-7) = 46$.

Hence $a = 53$.

Alternatively:

$t_2 = 46 \Rightarrow a + d = 46 \quad (1)$

$t_4 = 32 \Rightarrow a + 3d = 32 \quad (2)$

$(2) - (1)$ gives $2d = -14$ and so $d = -7$.

Question 68 C

Use $S_n = \frac{n}{2}\left[2a + (n-1)d\right]$ with $a = -18, d = 10$ and $n = 12$.

$$S_{12} = \frac{12}{2}\left[(2)(-18) + (12-1)(10)\right]$$
$$= 444$$

Question 69 B

For a geometric sequence, the common ratio, r, is given by

$r = \frac{t_k}{t_{k-1}}$ where $k > 1$.

The sequence in alternative **B** does not have a common ratio.

$$\frac{1.5}{1} \neq \frac{1.25}{1.5} \neq \frac{1.125}{1.25}$$

The other sequences are geometric.

Alternative **A**: $r = 0.5$

Alternative **C**: $r = 1$

Alternative **D**: $r = -\frac{1}{3}$

Alternative **E**: $r = 2^2$

Question 70 C

As each successive term is 25% of the value of the previous term,
$r = 0.25$.

Use $S_\infty = \frac{a}{1-r}$ with $a = 60$ and $r = 0.25$.

$$S_\infty = \frac{60}{1 - 0.25}$$
$$= 80$$

Question 71 D

This is a geometric sequence with $r = 1 + 0.3 = 1.3$.

At 9 am Monday there were 200 flies.

At 9 am Tuesday, there will be $200 \times 1.3 = 260$ flies.

At 9 am Wednesday, there will be $200 \times 1.3 \times 1.3 \approx 338$ flies.

Alternatively:

Use $t_n = ar^{n-1}$ with $a = 200$, $r = 1.3$ and $n = 3$.

$t_3 = 200 \times 1.3^2 = 338$

Question 72 A

The ladder looks like this:

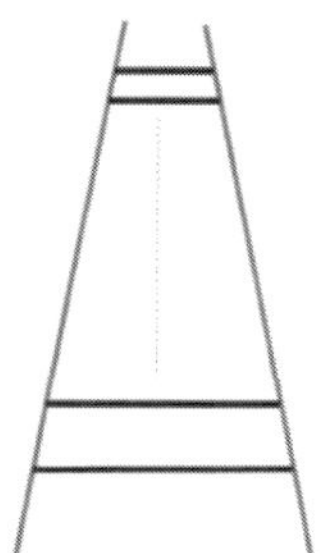

Each rung is 2 cm shorter than the last.

The lengths in cm are: 50, 48, 46, ...

This is an arithmetic sequence with $a = 50$ and $d = -2$.

The sum of n terms is given by

$S_n = \frac{n}{2}\left(2a + (n-1)d\right)$.

There are 10 steps so the sum is given by

$$S_{10} = \frac{10}{2}\left(2 \times 50 + (10-1) \times -2\right)$$
$$= 5(100 - 18)$$
$$= 410$$

The total length of wood required is 410 cm.

Question 73 D

$$w_{n+1} = 4w_n$$
$$w_3 = 4w_2 = 4\times 12 = 48$$
$$w_4 = 4w_3 = 4\times 48 = 192$$

The fourth term, w_4, is 192.

Question 74 A

The sequence values can be generated from the recurrence relation as follows:

$$L_0 = 37$$
$$L_1 = L_0 + C = 37 + C$$
$$L_2 = L_1 + C = (37+C)+C = 37+2C$$

Since $L_2 = 25$, this means that $37+2C = 25$.

Hence $C = -6$.

Question 75

a. Linking terms in both sequences:

$ar = a + d \quad (1)$

$ar^3 = a + 2d \quad (2)$

$2\times(1)-(2)$ gives:

$$2ar - ar^3 = a$$
$$ar^3 - 2ar + a = 0$$
$$a\left(r^3 - 2r + 1\right) = 0$$

As $a \neq 0$, $r^3 - 2r + 1 = 0$.

b. Expand $(r-1)\left(r^2+br+c\right)$.

$$\begin{aligned}(r-1)\left(r^2+br+c\right) &= r^3 + br^2 + cr - r^2 - br - c\\ &= r^3 + (b-1)r^2 + (c-b)r - c\end{aligned}$$

Equating coefficients:

$$r^3 - 2r + 1 = r^3 + (b-1)r^2 + (c-b)r - c$$

So $c = -1$ and $b - 1 = 0 \Rightarrow b = 1$.

So $r^3 - 2r + 1 = (r-1)\left(r^2+r-1\right)$.

c. $(r-1)\left(r^2+r-1\right) = 0$

As the sum of the geometric sequence is convergent, then $-1 < r < 1$ and $r - 1 \neq 0$.

Hence attempt to solve $r^2 + r - 1 = 0$.

$$\begin{aligned}r &= \frac{-1\pm\sqrt{1^2-4(1)(-1)}}{2}\\ &= \frac{-1\pm\sqrt{5}}{2}\end{aligned}$$

As $-1 < r < 1$, we reject $r = \frac{-1-\sqrt{5}}{2}$.

So $r = \frac{-1+\sqrt{5}}{2}$.

d. $\frac{a}{1-r} = 3+\sqrt{5}$

As $r = \frac{-1+\sqrt{5}}{2}$, $a = \left(1-\left(\frac{-1+\sqrt{5}}{2}\right)\right)\left(3+\sqrt{5}\right)$

$$\begin{aligned}a &= \left(\frac{3-\sqrt{5}}{2}\right)\left(3+\sqrt{5}\right)\\ &= \frac{1}{2}(9-5)\\ &= 2\end{aligned}$$

Question 76

a. Use $t_n = ar^{n-1}$ with $a = 10, r = 0.8$ and $n = 5$.

$$\begin{aligned}t_5 &= 10(0.8)^4\\ &= 4.096\end{aligned}$$

b. Use $S_n = \frac{a\left(1-r^n\right)}{1-r}$ with $a = 10, r = 0.8$ and $n = 25$.

$$\begin{aligned}S_{25} &= \frac{10\left(1-0.8^{25}\right)}{1-0.8}\\ &= 49.8111...\end{aligned}$$

$S_{25} = 49.8$ (correct to one decimal place)

c. Use $S_\infty = \frac{a}{1-r}$ with $a = 10$ and $r = 0.8$.

$$\begin{aligned}S_\infty &= \frac{10}{1-0.8}\\ &= 50\end{aligned}$$

Use $S_n = \frac{a\left(1-r^n\right)}{1-r}$ with $a = 10$ and $r = 0.8$.

$$\begin{aligned}S_n &= \frac{10\left(1-0.8^n\right)}{1-0.8}\\ &= 50\left(1-0.8^n\right)\end{aligned}$$

$$S_\infty - S_n < 0.01$$
$$50 - 50\left(1-0.8^n\right) < 0.01$$

Solving for n gives $n > 38.169...$.

Hence $n = 39$.

Question 77

a. From the first three terms of the sequence, form the following system of linear equations:

$5 = 4a + b \quad (1)$

$7 = 5a + b \quad (2)$

$(2)-(1)$ gives $a = 2$

Substituting $a = 2$ into (1) and solving gives $b = -3$.

So $t_{n+1} = 2t_n - 3,\ t_1 = 4$.

b. Use $t_4 = 2t_3 - 3$.

$$\begin{aligned} t_4 &= 2(7) - 3 \\ &= 11 \end{aligned}$$

c. Use $t_n = a^{n-1}t_1 + \dfrac{b\left(a^{n-1}-1\right)}{a-1}$ with $n = 4, a = 2$ and $b = -3$.

$$\begin{aligned} t_4 &= 2^{4-1}(4) - \frac{3\left(2^{4-1}-1\right)}{2-1} \\ &= 32 - 3(7) \\ &= 11 \end{aligned}$$

Question 78

a. Use $t_n = a^{n-1}t_1 + \dfrac{b\left(a^{n-1}-1\right)}{a-1}$ with $a = 3$ and $b = 1$.

$$\begin{aligned} t_n &= 3^{n-1}(2) + \frac{1\left(3^{n-1}-1\right)}{3-1} \\ &= 2\left(3^{n-1}\right) + \frac{1}{2}\left(3^{n-1}\right) - \frac{1}{2} \\ &= \frac{5}{2}\left(3^{n-1}\right) - \frac{1}{2} \end{aligned}$$

So $A = \dfrac{5}{2}$ and $B = -\dfrac{1}{2}$.

b. Use $t_n = \dfrac{5}{2}\left(3^{n-1}\right) - \dfrac{1}{2}$ with $n = 1, 2, 3, 4$.

$$t_1 = \frac{5}{2}\left(3^{1-1}\right) - \frac{1}{2} = \frac{5}{2} - \frac{1}{2} = 2$$

$$t_2 = \frac{5}{2}\left(3^{2-1}\right) - \frac{1}{2} = \frac{15}{2} - \frac{1}{2} = 7$$

$$t_3 = \frac{5}{2}\left(3^{3-1}\right) - \frac{1}{2} = \frac{45}{2} - \frac{1}{2} = 22$$

$$t_4 = \frac{5}{2}\left(3^{4-1}\right) - \frac{1}{2} = \frac{135}{2} - \frac{1}{2} = 67$$

The first four terms are $2, 7, 22, 67$.

c. As n becomes very large, $\dfrac{5}{2}\left(3^{n-1}\right)$ becomes very large.

So $t_n \to \infty$.

Question 79

a. From $A_{n+1} = rA_n - d,\ A_1 = a$:

$A_1 = 60\,000$ and so $a = 60\,000$ (initial amount borrowed)

$d = 550$ (monthly repayments)

b. $r = 1 + \dfrac{8.5}{12 \times 100} = 1.0070833...$

c. Use $A_n = r^{n-1}A_1 - \dfrac{d\left(r^{n-1}-1\right)}{r-1}$ with $A_1 = 60\,000$, $r = 1.0070833...$ and $d = 550$.

$$A_n = 60\,000(1.0070833...)^{n-1} - \frac{550\left((1.0070833...)^{n-1}-1\right)}{0.0070833...}$$

d. When the loan is paid off, $A_n = 0$.

Solving $A_n = 0$ for n gives $n = 210.907...$.

Now $A_1 = 60\,000,\ A_{210} = 495.85$ and $A_{211} = -50.64$.

As $A_{210} = 495.85\ (< 550)$, 209 repayments of \$550 are not sufficient to pay off the loan.

Hence 210 repayments are required.

Alternatively, a spreadsheet can be used to determine the number of repayments.

Note: In practice, it is usual to add the final amount owing (\$495.85) to \$550 to give \$1045.85, which is taken to be the final repayment.

Question 80

a. From $C_{n+1} = rC_n - d$:

$r = 1 + 0.1 = 1.1$ and $d = 50$

So $C_{n+1} = 1.1C_n - 50,\ C_1 = 600$.

b. Use $C_n = r^{n-1}C_1 - \dfrac{d\left(r^{n-1}-1\right)}{r-1}$ with $C_1 = 600,\ r = 1.1$ and $d = 50$.

$$\begin{aligned} C_n &= 600(1.1)^{n-1} - \frac{50\left(1.1^{n-1}-1\right)}{1.1-1} \\ &= 600(1.1)^{n-1} - 500(1.1)^{n-1} + 500 \\ &= 100(1.1)^{n-1} + 500 \end{aligned}$$

After 5 years:

$$\begin{aligned} C_6 &= 100(1.1)^5 + 500 \\ &\approx 661 \end{aligned}$$

c. Find the least value of n such that $C_n > 1000$.

Solving $C_n > 1000$ for n gives $n > 17.886...$.

By the start of the 18th year, the number of carp will first exceed 1000.

Alternatively, a spreadsheet can be used to determine the least value of n.

d. Let E_n be the number of carp in the dam at the start of the nth year.

$E_{n+1} = 1.1E_n - 75$, $E_1 = 600$

e. Use $E_n = r^{n-1}E_1 - \dfrac{d\left(r^{n-1}-1\right)}{r-1}$ with $E_1 = 600$, $r = 1.1$ and $d = 75$.

$$\begin{aligned} E_n &= 600(1.1)^{n-1} - \frac{75\left(1.1^{n-1}-1\right)}{1.1-1} \\ &= 600(1.1)^{n-1} - 750(1.1)^{n-1} + 750 \\ &= 750 - 150(1.1)^{n-1} \end{aligned}$$

Find the least value of n such that $E_n \le 0$.

Solving $E_n \le 0$ for n gives $n \ge 17.886...$.

Carp will disappear from the dam during the 17th year.

Alternatively, a spreadsheet can be used to determine the least value of n.

f. Let F_n be the number of carp in the dam at the start of the nth year.

$F_{n+1} = 1.1F_n - 60$, $F_1 = 600$

Use $F_n = r^{n-1}F_1 - \dfrac{d\left(r^{n-1}-1\right)}{r-1}$ with $F_1 = 600$, $r = 1.1$ and $d = 60$.

$$\begin{aligned} F_n &= 600(1.1)^{n-1} - \frac{60\left(1.1^{n-1}-1\right)}{1.1-1} \\ &= 600(1.1)^{n-1} - 600(1.1)^{n-1} + 600 \\ &= 600 \end{aligned}$$

$F_n = 600$ for all n

The model predicts that the number of carp will remain at 600.

Solutions: A5

Question 81 D

$$\frac{{}^nP_r}{{}^nP_{r-1}} = \frac{n!}{(n-r)!} \div \frac{n!}{(n-r+1)!}$$
$$= \frac{n!}{(n-r)!} \times \frac{(n-r+1)(n-r)!}{n!}$$
$$= n-r+1$$

Question 82 D

There are ${}^4C_3 = 4$ ways of selecting three vowels and ${}^4C_1 = 4$ ways of selecting one consonant, so there are 16 ways of selecting exactly three vowels (and one consonant).

Four letters can be chosen from eight in ${}^8C_4 = 70$ ways.

So the required probability is $\frac{16}{70} = \frac{8}{35}$.

Question 83 B

The inclusion-exclusion principle allows you to count the number of elements in a union of sets.

Let B be the set of Biology students, C the set of Chemistry students and P the set of Physics students. Then:

$$|B \cup C \cup P| = |B| + |C| + |P| - |B \cap C| - |B \cap P| - |C \cap P| + |B \cap C \cap P|$$

$= 7+10+10-3-4-5+1$

$= 16$

So the number of students who study none of these subjects is $18-16=2$.

Question 84 C

More girls than boys in the group of three means either all girls or two girls and one boy.

An all-girl group is obtained by choosing three girls from the five available in ${}^5C_3 = 10$ ways.

A group consisting of two girls and one boy is obtained by choosing two girls from the five girls available and one boy from the four boys available.

This can be done in ${}^5C_2 \times {}^4C_1 = 10 \times 4 = 40$ ways.

So the number of groups is $10+40=50$.

Question 85 E

For a set of 10 elements, there are 2^{10} subsets.

There are ${}^{10}C_1 = 10$ subsets consisting of one element and ${}^{10}C_0 = 1$ subset consisting of no elements.

So the number of subsets is $2^{10} - 11$.

Question 86 B

The number of possible lamb curry types for the given conditions are one lamb and three chicken or two lamb and two chicken. So:

${}^3C_1 \times {}^4C_3 = 12$ ways of choosing one lamb and three chicken curries;

${}^3C_2 \times {}^4C_2 = 18$ ways of choosing two lamb and two chicken curries.

So the number of different possible selections is $12+18=30$.

Question 87

There are 50 positive odd numbers less than 100 (namely 1, 3, 5, ..., 99).

Some of these can be paired to make a total of 102: 3 & 99, 5 &97 and so on.

Using this idea, partition the 50 numbers into subsets, where all but the first and last are subsets of size two whose elements sum to 102:

$\{1\}, \{3,99\}, \{5,97\}, \ldots, \{49,53\}, \{51\}$.

There are 26 subsets altogether and John was asked to choose 27 distinct odd numbers.

At most 26 of John's numbers can be in different subsets.

Hence at least two of John's numbers must lie in the same subset and therefore they will have a sum of 102, so Peter's claim is correct.

Question 88

a. $7! = 5040$

b. There are $4!$ ways of seating the 4 girls together and $3!$ ways of seating the 3 boys together.

Also, either the girls are seated to the left and the boys to the right or vice versa.

Thus the total number of arrangements is equal to $2 \times 4! \times 3! = 288$.

c. The girls and boys must alternate as follows: G B G B G B G.

There are $4!$ ways of seating the 4 girls and $3!$ ways of seating the 3 boys.

Thus the total number of arrangements is equal to $4! \times 3! = 144$.

Question 89

The generalized pigeonhole principle states that if $kn+1$ objects are placed in n boxes, then some box contains at least $k+1$ objects.

In this situation, $k=2$ and $n=7$, i.e. there are $2\times7+1=15$ people and 7 weekdays.

Hence at least $2+1=3$ people were born on the same day of the week.

(Alternatively, from first principles, there are 7 weekdays so if each contains just two people born on that day, the total number of people comes to 14.

Then the 15th person must join one of the groups of two.)

Question 90

$$\begin{aligned}\text{LHS} &= {}^nC_r + {}^nC_{r-1}\\ &= \frac{n!}{(n-r)!r!}+\frac{n!}{(n-r+1)!(r-1)!}\\ &= n!\left(\frac{n+1-r}{r!(n+1-r)!}+\frac{r}{r!(n+1-r)!}\right)\\ &= \frac{n!(n+1)}{r!(n+1-r)!}\\ &= \frac{(n+1)!}{r!(n+1-r)!}\\ &= {}^{n+1}C_r\\ &= \text{RHS}\end{aligned}$$

Question 91

a. Let A be the set of Accounting students and B the set of Biology students. Then:

$$\begin{aligned}|A\cup B| &= |A|+|B|-|A\cap B|\\ &= 30+35-20\\ &= 45\end{aligned}$$

b. The number who study neither subject is the total number of students less the number who study at least one subject.

So using part **a**, this is $110-45=65$.

Question 92

a. There are 9 cards that can fill the 1st position.

And 8 cards that can fill the 2nd position.

And 7 cards that can fill the 3rd position.

And 6 cards that can fill the 4th position.

Using the multiplication principle there are $9\times8\times7\times6=3024$ 4-digit numbers that can be formed.

Alternatively:

The number of ways of arranging 4 cards from 9 cards is ${}^9P_4=\frac{9!}{(9-4)!}$.

$$\begin{aligned}{}^9P_4 &= \frac{9\times8\times7\times6\times5!}{5!}\\ &= 9\times8\times7\times6\\ &= 3024\end{aligned}$$

b. Deal with the restriction first.

There are 5 cards displaying an odd number.

Hence there are 5 ways of filling the 4th position.

There are 8 cards that can fill the 1st position.

And 7 cards that can fill the 2nd position.

And 6 cards that can fill the 3rd position.

Using the multiplication principle there are $8\times7\times6\times5=1680$ odd 4-digit numbers that can be formed.

Alternatively:

The number of arrangements is ${}^8P_3\times5=\frac{8!}{(8-3)!}\times5$.

$$\begin{aligned}{}^8P_3\times5 &= \frac{8\times7\times6\times5!}{5!}\times5\\ &= 8\times7\times6\times5\\ &= 1680\end{aligned}$$

c. At least 3 odd digits means either 3 odd digits or 4 odd digits.

3 odd digits:

There are ${}^5C_3=10$ ways of selecting 3 odd digits and ${}^4C_1=4$ ways of selecting 1 even digit.

There are $10\times4=40$ ways of selecting exactly 3 odd digits (and 1 even digit).

4 odd digits:

There are ${}^5C_4=5$ ways of selecting 4 odd digits.

4 digits can be selected from 9 in ${}^9C_4=126$ ways.

The required probability is $\frac{40+5}{126}=\frac{5}{14}$.

d. There are two possible cases.

$9+8+7+4=28$ and $9+8+6+5=28$

The required probability is $\frac{2}{126}=\frac{1}{63}$.

Question 93

There are 4 distinct letters, G, U, E and S.

Omitting each of these letters in turn leaves 6 letters.

Case 1: Omitting an S leaves 2 Es and 2 Ss.

The number of 6-letter words is $\frac{6!}{2!2!} = 180$.

Case 2: Omitting an E leaves 3 Ss.

The number of 6-letter words is $\frac{6!}{3!} = 120$.

Case 3: Omitting G or U leaves 2 Es and 3Ss.

The number of 6-letter words is $\frac{6!}{3!2!} \times 2 = 120$.

The total number of 6-letter words is $180 + 120 + 120 = 420$.

Question 94

Let X, Y and Z be the sets of integers from 1 to 200 divisible by 2, 3 and 5 respectively. Thus:

$X = \{2, 4, ..., 200\}$ so $|X| = 100$

$Y = \{3, 6, ..., 198\}$ so $|Y| = 66$

$Z = \{5, 10, ..., 200\}$ so $|Z| = 40$

$X \cap Y = \{6, 12, ..., 198\}$ so $|X \cap Y| = 33$

$X \cap Z = \{10, 20, ..., 200\}$ so $|X \cap Z| = 20$

$Y \cap Z = \{15, 30, ..., 195\}$ so $|Y \cap Z| = 13$

$X \cap Y \cap Z = \{30, 60, ..., 180\}$ so $|X \cap Y \cap Z| = 6$

Using the inclusion-exclusion principle:

$$\begin{aligned} |X \cup Y \cup Z| &= |X| + |Y| + |Z| \\ &\quad - |X \cap Y| - |X \cap Z| - |Y \cap Z| \\ &\quad + |X \cap Y \cap Z| \end{aligned}$$

$$\begin{aligned} &= 100 + 66 + 40 - 33 - 20 - 13 + 6 \\ &= 146 \end{aligned}$$

So the number of integers from 1 to 200 inclusive not divisible by 2, 3 or 5 is equal to $200 - 146 = 54$.

Question 95

$${}^{n+1}P_r = {}^nP_r + r \times {}^nP_{r-1}$$

$$\text{LHS} = {}^{n+1}P_r = \frac{(n+1)!}{(n+1-r)!}$$

$$\begin{aligned} \text{RHS} &= {}^nP_r + r \times {}^nP_{r-1} \\ &= \frac{n!}{(n-r)!} + r \times \frac{n!}{(n-(r-1))!} \\ &= \frac{n!}{(n-r)!} + r \times \frac{n!}{(n+1-r)!} \\ &= \frac{n!}{(n-r)!} + \frac{r}{n+1-r} \times \frac{n!}{(n-r)!} \\ &= \frac{n!}{(n-r)!}\left(1 + \frac{r}{n+1-r}\right) \\ &= \frac{n!}{(n-r)!}\left(\frac{(n+1-r)+r}{n+1-r}\right) \\ &= \frac{n!}{(n-r)!}\left(\frac{n+1}{n+1-r}\right) \\ &= \frac{(n+1)!}{(n+1-r)!} \\ &= {}^{n+1}P_r \\ &= \text{LHS} \end{aligned}$$

So ${}^{n+1}P_r = {}^nP_r + r \times {}^nP_{r-1}$.

Solutions: A6

Question 96 D

Given $A=\begin{bmatrix} a & b \\ c & d \end{bmatrix}$, if $ad=bc$ then $\det A = ad-bc=0$.

Check each alternative in turn:

$ad \neq bc$ in each of alternatives **A**, **B**, **C** and **E**.

In alternative **D**, $3\times 4=6\times 2$.

Question 97 B

From the table, the following equations can be constructed:

$5c+7r+6s+8w=160$
$8c+6r+9s+7w=172$
$7c+8r+7s+6w=165$
$8c+8r+5s+5w=162$

Represented as a matrix equation:

$$\begin{bmatrix} 5 & 7 & 6 & 8 \\ 8 & 6 & 9 & 7 \\ 7 & 8 & 7 & 6 \\ 8 & 8 & 5 & 5 \end{bmatrix}\begin{bmatrix} c \\ r \\ s \\ w \end{bmatrix}=\begin{bmatrix} 160 \\ 172 \\ 165 \\ 162 \end{bmatrix}$$

The solution to this matrix equation can be found by evaluating:

$$\begin{bmatrix} c \\ r \\ s \\ w \end{bmatrix}=\begin{bmatrix} 5 & 7 & 6 & 8 \\ 8 & 6 & 9 & 7 \\ 7 & 8 & 7 & 6 \\ 8 & 8 & 5 & 5 \end{bmatrix}^{-1}\begin{bmatrix} 160 \\ 172 \\ 165 \\ 162 \end{bmatrix}$$
$$=\begin{bmatrix} 8 \\ 6 \\ 1 \\ 9 \end{bmatrix}$$

Question 98 C

For matrix addition, we require the matrices to have the same dimension.

$\begin{bmatrix} 8 \\ 12 \end{bmatrix}+\begin{bmatrix} 4 \\ 2 \end{bmatrix}$ is defined as both matrices are 2×1.

$\begin{bmatrix} 8 & 0 \\ 12 & 0 \end{bmatrix}+\begin{bmatrix} 4 & 0 \\ 0 & 2 \end{bmatrix}$ is defined as both matrices are 2×2.

Question 99 D

$$6\times 7+6\times 8=\begin{bmatrix} 6 & 6 \end{bmatrix}\times\begin{bmatrix} 7 \\ 8 \end{bmatrix}=\begin{bmatrix} 90 \end{bmatrix}$$

Alternative **D** creates a 1×1 matrix which gives the total cost of the rides.

Alternative **A** creates a 1×2 matrix which gives the cost of The Big Dipper and The Terror Train rides separately (not as a single total).

Alternatives **B** and **C** are not possible, since the number of columns in the first matrix do not match the number of rows in the second matrix.

Alternative **E** creates a 2×2 matrix which does not give the total cost.

Question 100 E

All the rules produce $p_{11}=3$.

Consider $p_{12}=2$:

Alternative **A**: $p_{12}=4-2=2$

Alternative **E**: $p_{12}=2(1)-2+2=2$

Alternatives **B**, **C** and **D** each give $p_{12}\neq 2$.

Consider $p_{22}=4$:

Alternative **A**: $p_{22}=4-2=2\neq 4$

Alternative **E**: $p_{22}=2(2)-2+2=4$

The rule in alternative **E** works for all elements in P.

Alternatively:

Let $ai+bj+c=p_{ij}$ and form 3 linear equations in a,b and c.

For example,

$p_{11}=3 \Rightarrow a+b+c=3$

$p_{12}=2 \Rightarrow a+2b+c=2$

$p_{21}=5 \Rightarrow 2a+b+c=5$

Solving this system of linear equations gives $a=2, b=-1$ and $c=2$.

Question 101 B

Consider each alternative in turn:

Alternative **A** is incorrect as equation 3 should be $2w-2y=-8$.

Alternative **B** is correct.

Alternative **C** is incorrect as equation 1 should be $2v+2w-2y=2$.

Alternative **D** is incorrect as equation 4 should be $2v+2w-2x=4$.

Alternative **E** is incorrect as equation 2 should be $2v-2x=6$.

Question 102 E

Element q_{41} is obtained by multiplying the 4th row of matrix A by the 1st column of matrix B.

This gives $4\times 2+5\times 4$.

Question 103 D

$P^n \times W = W$ is only true if $P^n = I$.

Testing n values between 2 and 5 inclusive shows that $n = 4$ gives an identity matrix, I.

That is,

$$\begin{bmatrix} 0 & 0 & 1 & 0 & 0 \\ 0 & 0 & 0 & 0 & 1 \\ 0 & 1 & 0 & 0 & 0 \\ 0 & 0 & 0 & 1 & 0 \\ 1 & 0 & 0 & 0 & 0 \end{bmatrix}^4 = \begin{bmatrix} 1 & 0 & 0 & 0 & 0 \\ 0 & 1 & 0 & 0 & 0 \\ 0 & 0 & 1 & 0 & 0 \\ 0 & 0 & 0 & 1 & 0 \\ 0 & 0 & 0 & 0 & 1 \end{bmatrix}$$

Question 104 B

Let $M = \begin{bmatrix} m_{11} & m_{12} & m_{13} \\ m_{21} & m_{22} & m_{23} \\ m_{31} & m_{32} & m_{33} \end{bmatrix}$.

Using the rule $m_{ij} = 3i + 2j$ gives:

$$M = \begin{bmatrix} 3(1)+2(1) & 3(1)+2(2) & 3(1)+2(3) \\ 3(2)+2(1) & 3(2)+2(2) & 3(2)+2(3) \\ 3(3)+2(1) & 3(3)+2(2) & 3(3)+2(3) \end{bmatrix}$$

$$= \begin{bmatrix} 5 & 7 & 9 \\ 8 & 10 & 12 \\ 11 & 13 & 15 \end{bmatrix}$$

Question 105 A

In matrix form, the system of linear equations can be represented as:

$$\begin{bmatrix} a & 4 \\ 18 & b \end{bmatrix} \begin{bmatrix} x \\ y \end{bmatrix} = \begin{bmatrix} 10 \\ 6 \end{bmatrix}$$

Let $A = \begin{bmatrix} a & 4 \\ 18 & b \end{bmatrix}$.

The system of equations does not have a unique solution if $\det A = 0$.

Hence there is no unique solution if

$$\det A = ab - 4 \times 18 = 0$$
$$ab - 72 = 0$$
$$ab = 72$$

This is only true for alternative **A** $(2 \times 36 = 72)$.

Question 106

a. Matrix Q is of order 3 by 2.

b. The sum of column 2 is:

$50 + 20 + 40 = 110$

c. Matrix P is a 1 by 3 row matrix.

Given that matrix $P \times L$ is a 1 by 1 matrix, then matrix L must be a 3 by 1 matrix that represents the number of full parking spaces in areas A, B and C.

$$L = \begin{bmatrix} 50 \\ 20 \\ 40 \end{bmatrix} \begin{matrix} A \\ B \\ C \end{matrix}$$

Question 107

a. As A is singular, $\det A = 0$.

$(k)(1) - (3)(-2) = 0 \Rightarrow k = -6$

b. $A^{-1} = \dfrac{1}{k+6} \begin{bmatrix} 1 & -3 \\ 2 & k \end{bmatrix}$

$AX = B \Rightarrow X = A^{-1}B$ where $X = \begin{bmatrix} x \\ y \end{bmatrix}$ and $B = \begin{bmatrix} 1 \\ -1 \end{bmatrix}$

$$\begin{bmatrix} x \\ y \end{bmatrix} = \frac{1}{k+6} \begin{bmatrix} 1 & -3 \\ 2 & k \end{bmatrix} \begin{bmatrix} 1 \\ -1 \end{bmatrix}$$
$$= \frac{1}{k+6} \begin{bmatrix} (1)(1)+(-3)(-1) \\ (2)(1)+(k)(-1) \end{bmatrix}$$
$$= \frac{1}{k+6} \begin{bmatrix} 4 \\ 2-k \end{bmatrix}$$

So $x = \dfrac{4}{k+6}$ and $y = \dfrac{2-k}{k+6}$.

Question 108

a. $\text{LHS} = AB\left(A^{-1}B\right)^{-1}$

$$= ABB^{-1}\left(A^{-1}\right)^{-1}$$
$$= AIA$$
$$= A^2$$
$$= \text{RHS}$$

Here $\left(A^{-1}B\right)^{-1} = B^{-1}\left(A^{-1}\right)^{-1}$ and $\left(A^{-1}\right)^{-1} = A$.

b. $\text{LHS} = B(AB)^{-1} A - I$

$$= BB^{-1}A^{-1}A - I$$
$$= I^2 - I$$
$$= O$$
$$= \text{RHS}$$

Here $(AB)^{-1} = B^{-1}A^{-1}$.

Question 109

a. $AB = \begin{bmatrix} 2 & 1 & 1 \\ 0 & 3 & 4 \\ 6 & 0 & 1 \end{bmatrix}\begin{bmatrix} 3 & -1 & 1 \\ 24 & -4 & -8 \\ -18 & 6 & 6 \end{bmatrix}$

$$= \begin{bmatrix} 6+24-18 & -2-4+6 & 2-8+6 \\ 0+72-72 & 0-12+24 & 0-24+24 \\ 18+0-18 & -6+0+6 & 6+0+6 \end{bmatrix}$$

$$= \begin{bmatrix} 12 & 0 & 0 \\ 0 & 12 & 0 \\ 0 & 0 & 12 \end{bmatrix}$$

$= 12I$

b. $AB = 12I$

$$A^{-1}AB = 12A^{-1}I$$
$$B = 12A^{-1}$$
$$A^{-1} = \frac{1}{12}B$$

Now $AX = C$

where $A = \begin{bmatrix} 2 & 1 & 1 \\ 0 & 3 & 4 \\ 6 & 0 & 1 \end{bmatrix}$, $X = \begin{bmatrix} x \\ y \\ z \end{bmatrix}$ and $C = \begin{bmatrix} -1 \\ -7 \\ 8 \end{bmatrix}$.

$AX = C \Rightarrow X = A^{-1}C$ and $A^{-1} = \frac{1}{12}B$

So $X = \frac{1}{12}BC$.

$$X = \frac{1}{12}\begin{bmatrix} 3 & -1 & 1 \\ 24 & -4 & -8 \\ -18 & 6 & 6 \end{bmatrix}\begin{bmatrix} -1 \\ -7 \\ 8 \end{bmatrix}$$

$$= \begin{bmatrix} (3)(-1)+(-1)(-7)+(1)(8) \\ (24)(-1)+(-4)(-7)+(-8)(8) \\ (-18)(-1)+(6)(-7)+(6)(8) \end{bmatrix}$$

$$= \frac{1}{12}\begin{bmatrix} 12 \\ -60 \\ 24 \end{bmatrix}$$

$$= \begin{bmatrix} 1 \\ -5 \\ 2 \end{bmatrix}$$

So $x = 1, y = -5$ and $z = 2$.

Question 110

a. $A^2 = \begin{bmatrix} 2 & 1 \\ 7 & 4 \end{bmatrix}\begin{bmatrix} 2 & 1 \\ 7 & 4 \end{bmatrix}$

$$= \begin{bmatrix} 2\times2+1\times7 & 2\times1+1\times4 \\ 7\times2+4\times7 & 7\times1+4\times4 \end{bmatrix}$$

$$= \begin{bmatrix} 11 & 6 \\ 42 & 23 \end{bmatrix}$$

Substituting into $pI + qA + A^2 = O$:

$$p\begin{bmatrix} 1 & 0 \\ 0 & 1 \end{bmatrix} + q\begin{bmatrix} 2 & 1 \\ 7 & 4 \end{bmatrix} + \begin{bmatrix} 11 & 6 \\ 42 & 23 \end{bmatrix} = \begin{bmatrix} 0 & 0 \\ 0 & 0 \end{bmatrix}$$

By comparing the corresponding elements of the matrices on both sides we have 4 equations in p and q.

$$p + 2q + 11 = 0$$
$$q + 6 = 0$$
$$7q + 42 = 0$$
$$p + 4q + 23 = 0$$

Solving gives $p = 1$ and $q = -6$.

b. From part (a), $I - 6A + A^2 = O$.

$$I = 6A - A^2$$
$$= A(6I - A)$$

Hence A is non-singular and its inverse is $A^{-1} = 6I - A$.

$$A^{-1} = 6\begin{bmatrix} 1 & 0 \\ 0 & 1 \end{bmatrix} - \begin{bmatrix} 2 & 1 \\ 7 & 4 \end{bmatrix}$$

$$= \begin{bmatrix} 4 & -1 \\ -7 & 2 \end{bmatrix}$$

c. Pre-multiply both sides of $AX = \begin{bmatrix} 1 & 1 \\ -1 & 0 \end{bmatrix}$ by A^{-1}.

$$A^{-1}(AX) = A^{-1}\begin{bmatrix} 1 & 1 \\ -1 & 0 \end{bmatrix}$$

$$(A^{-1}A)X = \begin{bmatrix} 4 & -1 \\ -7 & 2 \end{bmatrix}\begin{bmatrix} 1 & 1 \\ -1 & 0 \end{bmatrix}$$

$$IX = \begin{bmatrix} (4)(1)+(-1)(-1) & (4)(1)+(-1)(0) \\ (-7)(1)+(2)(-1) & (-7)(1)+(2)(0) \end{bmatrix}$$

$$X = \begin{bmatrix} 5 & 4 \\ -9 & -7 \end{bmatrix}$$

Solutions: B1

Question 111 C

Phil must use a procedure with a probability of $\frac{1}{12}$ of success on each roll of the two dice.

Check each alternative in turn:

A: a sum of 12 (66) has probability $\frac{1}{36}$; no.

B: 2 ways out of 36 give a sum of 11 (56, 65) so this has probability $\frac{1}{18}$; no.

C: 3 ways out of 36 give a sum of 11 or more (56, 65, 66) so this has probability $\frac{1}{12}$; yes.

D: 4 ways out of 36 give a product of 12 (26, 34, 43, 62) so this has probability $\frac{1}{9}$; no.

E: 6 ways out of 36 give the same number (11, 22, …, 66) so this has probability $\frac{1}{6}$; no.

Question 112 E

The important point to remember is that in a simple random sample, each individual must have an equal chance of inclusion in the sample (and all subgroups of 100 must be possible).

Check each alternative in turn:

A: many voters will not use trains, so not all enrolled voters can be sampled: no.

B: many voters will not be in the white pages, so they cannot be selected; no.

C: only a limited number of subgroups of voters are possible; no.

D: only a limited number of subgroups of voters are possible as this forces the sample to have exactly 50 of each gender; no.

E: each voter has an equal chance of selection (and any subgroup is possible); yes.

Question 113 D

$$\begin{aligned}\mathrm{E}(X) &= \sum x\Pr(X=x)\\ &= -1\times p+0\times 2p+1\times(1-3p)\\ &= -p+1-3p\\ &= 1-4p\end{aligned}$$

$$\begin{aligned}\mathrm{E}(X^2) &= \sum x^2\Pr(X=x)\\ &= (-1)^2\times p+0^2\times 2p+1^2\times(1-3p)\\ &= p+1-3p\\ &= 1-2p\end{aligned}$$

$$\begin{aligned}\mathrm{Var}(X) &= \mathrm{E}(X^2)-[\mathrm{E}(X)]^2\\ &= 1-2p-(1-4p)^2\\ &= 6p-16p^2\end{aligned}$$

Question 114 D

$$\sum \Pr(X=x)=1$$

$$\begin{aligned}a+3a+5a+7a &= 1\\ 16a &= 1\\ a &= \frac{1}{16}\end{aligned}$$

$$\begin{aligned}\mathrm{E}(X) &= \sum x\Pr(X=x)\\ &= \left(0\times\frac{1}{16}\right)+\left(1\times\frac{3}{16}\right)+\left(2\times\frac{5}{16}\right)+\left(3\times\frac{7}{16}\right)\\ &= \frac{17}{8}\end{aligned}$$

Question 115 A

$$\begin{aligned}\mathrm{E}(X_1+X_2+X_3) &= \mathrm{E}(X_1)+\mathrm{E}(X_2)+\mathrm{E}(X_3)\\ &= \mu+\mu+\mu\\ &= 3\mu\end{aligned}$$

$$\begin{aligned}\mathrm{Var}(X_1+X_2+X_3) &= \mathrm{Var}(X_1)+\mathrm{Var}(X_2)+\mathrm{Var}(X_3)\\ &= \sigma^2+\sigma^2+\sigma^2\\ &= 3\sigma^2\end{aligned}$$

Question 116 B

Alternatives **A** and **E** are correct.

$$\begin{aligned}\mathrm{E}(X_1+X_2) &= \mathrm{E}(X_1)+\mathrm{E}(X_2)\\ &= \mu+\mu\\ &= 2\mu\\ &= 2\mathrm{E}(X)\end{aligned}$$

$$2\mathrm{E}(X)=\mathrm{E}(2X)$$

Alternative **B** is incorrect and alternative **C** is correct.

$$\begin{aligned}\mathrm{Var}(X_1+X_2) &= \mathrm{Var}(X_1)+\mathrm{Var}(X_2)\\ &= \sigma^2+\sigma^2\\ &= 2\sigma^2\\ &= 2\mathrm{Var}(X)\\ &\neq 4\mathrm{Var}(X)\end{aligned}$$

Alternative **D** is correct.

$$\begin{aligned}\mathrm{Var}(2X) &= 2^2\,\mathrm{Var}(X)\\ &= 4\mathrm{Var}(X)\end{aligned}$$

Question 117 C

The key idea is that there are population parameters (such as means of proportions) and samples that are used to provide statistics to estimate these parameters.

Question 118 C

If samples of size n are selected from a population with mean μ and standard deviation σ, then the sample mean $\bar{X}$ satisfies $\mathrm{E}(\bar{X})=\mu$ and $\mathrm{sd}(\bar{X})=\frac{\sigma}{\sqrt{n}}$.

As $\mathrm{E}(\bar{X})=27$, alternatives **B** and **E** can be disregarded.

Further, as $\mathrm{sd}(\bar{X})=\frac{9}{\sqrt{36}}=1.5$, alternatives **A** and **D** can be disregarded.

Alternative **C** is correct, $\mathrm{E}(\bar{X})=27$, $\mathrm{sd}(\bar{X})=1.5$.

Question 119 D

The population mean μ is constant for a given population.

Hence alternatives **A** and **C** can be disregarded.

The sample mean $\bar{x}$ varies from sample to sample.

Hence alternatives **B** and **E** can be disregarded.

Alternative **D** is correct.

Question 120

a. $\mu=20$

b. $\bar{x}=24$

Question 121

a. $\sum \Pr(X=x)=1$

$$0.2+0.6p^2+0.1+1-p+0.1=1$$
$$0.6p^2-p+0.4=0$$

Multiply both sides by 5:

$$3p^2-5p+2=0$$
$$(3p-2)(p-1)=0$$
$$p=\frac{2}{3},1$$

b. i. $\mathrm{E}(X)=\sum x\Pr(X=x)$

$$\begin{aligned}\mathrm{E}(X)&=\left(0\times\frac{2}{10}\right)+\left(1\times\frac{6}{10}\times\frac{4}{9}\right)+\left(2\times\frac{1}{10}\right)\\&\quad+\left(3\times\frac{1}{3}\right)+\left(4\times\frac{1}{10}\right)\\&=\frac{1}{30}(8+6+30+12)\\&=\frac{56}{30}\\&=\frac{28}{15}\end{aligned}$$

ii. $\Pr(X\geq \mathrm{E}(X))=\Pr\left(X\geq\frac{28}{15}\right)$

$$\begin{aligned}\Pr\left(X\geq\frac{28}{15}\right)&=\Pr(X\geq 2)\\&=0.1+\frac{1}{3}+0.1\\&=\frac{1}{10}+\frac{1}{3}+\frac{1}{10}\\&=\frac{16}{30}\\&=\frac{8}{15}\end{aligned}$$

Question 122

$$\begin{aligned}\mathrm{E}(X_1+2X_2+X_3)&=\mathrm{E}(X_1)+2\mathrm{E}(X_2)+\mathrm{E}(X_3)\\&=6+(2\times 6)+6\\&=24\end{aligned}$$

$$\begin{aligned}\mathrm{Var}(X_1+2X_2+X_3)&=\mathrm{Var}(X_1)+2^2\mathrm{Var}(X_2)+\mathrm{Var}(X_3)\\&=4+(4\times 4)+4\\&=24\end{aligned}$$

The standard deviation is $\sqrt{24}\left(=2\sqrt{6}\right)$.

Question 123

a. $\mathrm{E}(X)=\sum x\Pr(X=x)$

$$\begin{aligned}\mathrm{E}(X)&=\left(1\times\frac{1}{4}\right)+\left(2\times\frac{1}{4}\right)+\left(3\times\frac{1}{4}\right)+\left(4\times\frac{1}{4}\right)\\&=\frac{1}{4}(1+2+3+4)\\&=\frac{10}{4}\\&=\frac{5}{2}(=2.5)\end{aligned}$$

$$\mathrm{Var}(X)=\mathrm{E}(X^2)-[\mathrm{E}(X)]^2$$

$$\begin{aligned}\mathrm{E}(X^2)&=\left(1^2\times\frac{1}{4}\right)+\left(2^2\times\frac{1}{4}\right)+\left(3^2\times\frac{1}{4}\right)+\left(4^2\times\frac{1}{4}\right)\\&=\frac{1}{4}(1+4+9+16)\\&=\frac{30}{4}\\&=\frac{15}{2}(=7.5)\end{aligned}$$

From above, $\mathrm{E}(X)=\frac{5}{2}$.

$$\begin{aligned}\mathrm{Var}(X)&=\frac{30}{4}-\left(\frac{5}{2}\right)^2\\&=\frac{30}{4}-\frac{25}{4}(=7.5-6.25)\\&=\frac{5}{4}(=1.25)\end{aligned}$$

b. The sum $X_1 + X_2$ can take the values $2, 3, \ldots, 7, 8$.

There are 16 equally likely outcomes for pairs of numbers obtained.

One way of finding the probability of a value of $X_1 + X_2$ is to construct a table and count the number of associated pairs.

For example:

$$\begin{aligned}\Pr(X_1 + X_2 = 2) &= \Pr(X_1 = 1, X_2 = 1)\\ &= \frac{1}{4}\times\frac{1}{4}\\ &= \frac{1}{16}\end{aligned}$$

$$\begin{aligned}\Pr(X_1 + X_2 = 3) &= \Pr(X_1 = 1, X_2 = 2) + \Pr(X_1 = 2, X_2 = 1)\\ &= \left(\frac{1}{4}\times\frac{1}{4}\right)+\left(\frac{1}{4}\times\frac{1}{4}\right)\\ &= \frac{2}{16}\left(=\frac{1}{8}\right)\end{aligned}$$

Continuing in this way, the probability distribution of $X_1 + X_2$ is

$x_1 + x_2$	2	3	4	5	6	7	8
$\Pr(X_1 + X_2 = x_1 + x_2)$	$\frac{1}{16}$	$\frac{2}{16}$	$\frac{3}{16}$	$\frac{4}{16}$	$\frac{3}{16}$	$\frac{2}{16}$	$\frac{1}{16}$

c. The sum $X_1 + X_2$ can take the odd values $3, 5, 7$.

$$\begin{aligned}\Pr(X_1 + X_2 \text{ is odd}) &= \Pr(X_1 + X_2 = 3) + \Pr(X_1 + X_2 = 5)\\ &\quad + \Pr(X_1 + X_2 = 7)\\ &= \frac{2}{16}+\frac{4}{16}+\frac{2}{16}\\ &= \frac{1}{2}\end{aligned}$$

d. $\mathrm{E}(X_1 + X_2) = \sum (x_1 + x_2)\Pr(X = X_1 + X_2)$

$$\begin{aligned}\mathrm{E}(X_1 + X_2) &= \left(2\times\frac{1}{16}\right)+\left(3\times\frac{2}{16}\right)+\ldots+\left(7\times\frac{2}{16}\right)+\left(8\times\frac{1}{16}\right)\\ &= \frac{1}{16}(2+6+12+20+18+14+8)\\ &= \frac{80}{16}\\ &= 5\end{aligned}$$

Note that the mean of the sum is equal to the sum of the means.

$$\begin{aligned}\mathrm{E}(X_1 + X_2) &= \mathrm{E}(X_1) + \mathrm{E}(X_2)\\ &= 2.5 + 2.5\\ &= 5\end{aligned}$$

$$\mathrm{Var}(X_1 + X_2) = \mathrm{E}\left[(X_1 + X_2)^2\right] - \left[\mathrm{E}(X_1 + X_2)\right]^2$$

$$\begin{aligned}\mathrm{E}\left[(X_1 + X_2)^2\right] &= \left(2^2\times\frac{1}{16}\right)+\left(3^2\times\frac{2}{16}\right)+\ldots+\left(7^2\times\frac{2}{16}\right)+\left(8^2\times\frac{1}{16}\right)\\ &= \frac{1}{16}(4+18+48+100+108+98+64)\\ &= \frac{440}{16}\\ &= \frac{55}{2}(=27.5)\end{aligned}$$

From above, $\mathrm{E}(X_1 + X_2) = 5$.

$$\begin{aligned}\mathrm{Var}(X_1 + X_2) &= \frac{55}{2} - 5^2\\ &= \frac{5}{2}(=2.5)\end{aligned}$$

The variance of the sum is equal to the sum of the variances.

$$\begin{aligned}\mathrm{Var}(X_1 + X_2) &= \mathrm{Var}(X_1) + \mathrm{Var}(X_2)\\ &= 1.25 + 1.25\\ &= 2.5\end{aligned}$$

Note that $\mathrm{sd}(X_1 + X_2) \neq \mathrm{sd}(X_1) + \mathrm{sd}(X_2)$.

Question 124

a. $\bar{X} = \dfrac{X_1 + X_2 + \ldots + X_n}{n}$

where $X_1, X_2, \ldots, X_n$ are independent random variables with identical distributions to X.

$$\begin{aligned}\text{LHS} &= \mathrm{E}(\bar{X})\\ &= \mathrm{E}\left(\frac{X_1 + X_2 + \ldots + X_n}{n}\right)\\ &= \frac{1}{n}\mathrm{E}(X_1 + X_2 + \ldots + X_n)\\ &= \frac{1}{n}(\mathrm{E}(X_1) + \mathrm{E}(X_2) + \ldots + \mathrm{E}(X_n))\\ &= \frac{1}{n}(n\mu)\\ &= \mu\\ &= \text{RHS}\end{aligned}$$

b. $\text{Var}(\bar{X}) = \text{Var}\left(\frac{X_1 + X_2 + ... + X_n}{n}\right)$

where $X_1, X_2, ..., X_n$ are independent random variables with identical distributions to X.

$$\begin{aligned}
\text{LHS} &= \text{Var}(\bar{X}) \\
&= \text{Var}\left(\frac{X_1 + X_2 + ... + X_n}{n}\right) \\
&= \frac{1}{n^2}\text{Var}(X_1 + X_2 + ... + X_n) \\
&= \frac{1}{n^2}(\text{Var}(X_1) + \text{Var}(X_2) + ... + \text{Var}(X_n)) \\
&= \frac{1}{n^2}(n\sigma^2) \\
&= \frac{\sigma^2}{n} \\
&= \text{RHS}
\end{aligned}$$

Question 125

a. From the dotplot, 4 out of 50 samples have a sample mean of more than 21.

$$\Pr(\bar{X} \geq 21) \approx \frac{4}{50} = 0.08$$

b. From the dotplot, 42 out of 50 samples have a sample mean between 18.5 and 21.

$$\Pr(18.5 \leq \bar{X} \leq 21) \approx \frac{42}{50} = 0.84$$

Solutions: B2

Question 126 D

The area of the sector representing 'agree' will be 80% of the area of the circle.

Let the area be A.

$$A = \frac{80}{100} \times \pi \times 16^2$$
$$= 643.39... \text{ (mm}^2\text{)}$$

This is closest to 643 square millimetres.

Question 127 C

First calculate the distance along the ground from the base of the tower to A.

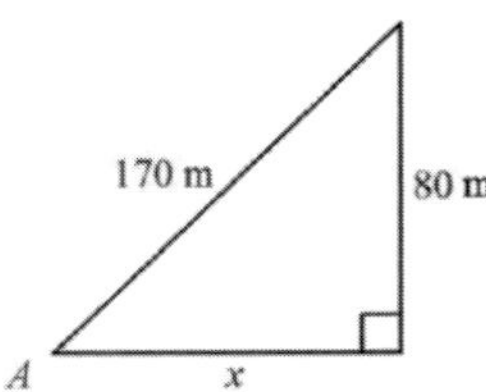

$$x = \sqrt{170^2 - 80^2}$$
$$= 150 \text{ (m)}$$

(Alternatively, you may recognise this as an 8-15-17 triangle multiplied by a scale factor of 10 and therefore $x = 15 \times 10 = 150$ (m).)

Now calculate the distance along the ground from the base of the tower to B.

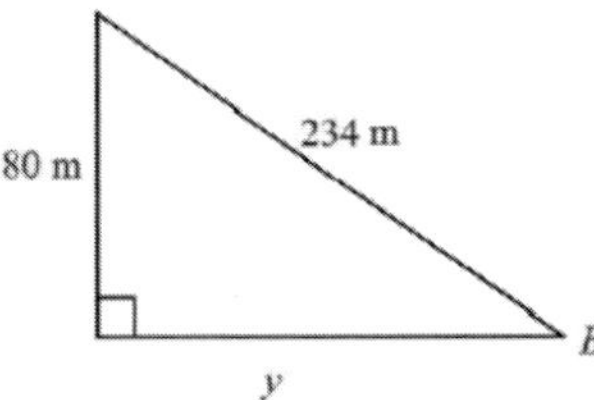

$$y = \sqrt{234^2 - 80^2}$$
$$= 219.899... \text{ (m)}$$

To find the distance between A and B, first use the bearings given to find the angle in the triangle at B.

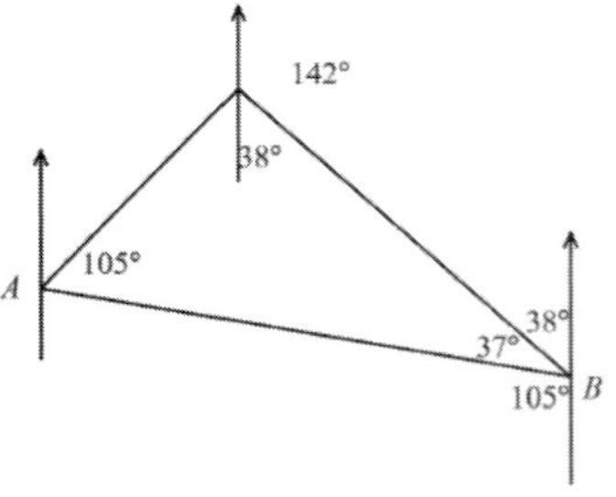

Angle B in the triangle shown is $142° - 105° = 37°$.

Now use the cosine rule to find the length AB.

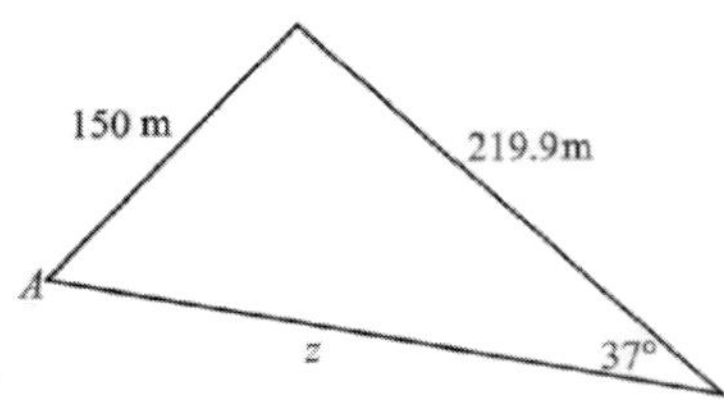

$$150^2 = z^2 + 219.9^2 - 2(219.9)\cos(37°)z$$

$z = 246$ (m) or $z = 105$ (m) (correct to the nearest metre)

The closest to either possible answer is 246 m.

The sine and cosine rules could also be used here.

Question 128 B

Rod walks 1400 m due east from the car park (*P*) to the lookout (*L*).

Rod then walks x m on a bearing of 240° to the cafe (*C*) then 700 m from the cafe to the car park.

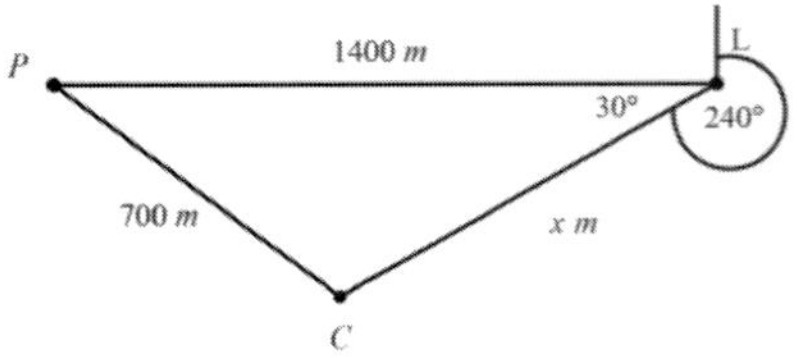

Use the cosine rule to find x.

$$700^2 = x^2 + 1400^2 - (2)(1400)\cos(30°)x$$
$$x = 1212.43...\text{(m)}$$

Correct to the nearest metre, Rod's return trip from the lookout to the car park is $1212 + 700 = 1912$ (m).

Lucia walks 1400 m due east from the car park (P) to the lookout (L).

Lucia then walks y m on a bearing of 290° to the swimming hole (S) then 950 m from the swimming hole to the car park.

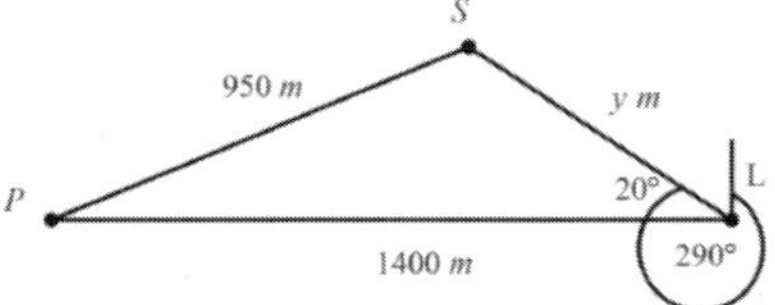

Use the cosine rule to find y.

$$950^2 = y^2 + 1400^2 - (2)(1400)\cos(20°)y$$
$$y = 495.06...(\text{m})$$

(Reject the solution $y = 2126.07...(\text{m})$ since the swimming hole is closer to the lookout than the car park.)

Correct to the nearest metre, Lucia's return trip from the lookout to the car park is $495 + 950 = 1445$ (m).

Rod walks $1912 - 1445 = 467$ (m) further than Lucia.

The sine rule could also be used to solve this question.

Question 129 A

A standard result that you should know is $\sin^2(\theta) + \cos^2(\theta) = 1$ for *any* value of θ.

So there is no need to evaluate the sin and cos terms, square and add.

Thus $\sin^2\left(\frac{3\pi}{4}\right) + \cos^2\left(\frac{3\pi}{4}\right) = 1$.

Question 130 B

$$\frac{1 - \cos^2(x)}{\tan(x)} = \sin^2(x) \div \tan(x)$$
$$= \sin^2(x) \div \frac{\sin(x)}{\cos(x)}$$
$$= \sin^2(x) \times \frac{\cos(x)}{\sin(x)}$$
$$= \sin(x)\cos(x)$$

Question 131 E

$$\frac{\cos\left(\frac{\pi}{2} - x\right)}{\sin\left(\frac{\pi}{2} - x\right)} = \frac{\sin(x)}{\cos(x)} = \tan(x)$$

as $\sin\left(\frac{\pi}{2} - x\right) = \cos(x)$ and $\cos\left(\frac{\pi}{2} - x\right) = \sin(x)$

(An alternative method is to express the fraction in terms of tan and then cot (the reciprocal of tan) together with the fact that $\tan\left(\frac{\pi}{2} - x\right) = \cot(x)$.)

Question 132 A

$$b = \cot(x) = \frac{\cos(x)}{\sin(x)} = \frac{-a}{\sin(x)}$$

$$\frac{b}{a} = -\frac{1}{\sin(x)} = \frac{1}{\sin(-x)} = \text{cosec}(-x)$$

Question 133

The area A of the sector of a circle is given by $A = \frac{1}{2}r^2\theta$, where θ is measured in radians.

Substituting the given values:

$$\frac{1}{2}(6)^2\theta = 50 \Rightarrow \theta = \frac{25}{9}$$

The arc length l is given by $l = r\theta$.

So $l = 6 \times \frac{25}{9} = \frac{50}{3} = 16\frac{2}{3}$ (cm).

Question 134

a. The area of triangle AOB is $\sqrt{3}$ cm².

$$\frac{1}{2} \times 2 \times 2 \times \sin(\theta) = \sqrt{3} \quad \left(A = \frac{1}{2}r^2\sin(\theta)\right)$$
$$\sin(\theta) = \frac{\sqrt{3}}{2}$$
$$\theta = \frac{\pi}{3} \text{ or } \frac{2\pi}{3}$$

Thus the other value for θ is $\frac{2\pi}{3}$.

b. $A = \frac{1}{2}r^2\theta$, so:

$$A = \frac{1}{2} \times 2 \times 2 \times \frac{\pi}{3}$$
$$= \frac{2\pi}{3} \text{ (cm}^2\text{)}$$

c. For the length of the arc AB:

$$l = r\theta = 2 \times \frac{\pi}{3} = \frac{2\pi}{3} \text{ (cm)}.$$

For the line segment AB, you should recognise that as $OA = OB$ (equal radii) and so $\theta = \frac{\pi}{3}$, OAB is an equilateral triangle, so $AB = 2$ cm.

(Alternatively, you could use the cosine rule.)

Thus the exact length of the perimeter of the minor segment is $2 + \frac{2\pi}{3}$ cm.

Question 135

a. Arc length l is given by $l = r\theta$, so:

$$9 = 5\theta \Rightarrow \theta = \frac{9}{5} = 1.8 \text{ (radians)}$$

Thus $\angle POQ = \frac{9}{5} = 1.8$ (radians).

b. To show ΔOPT is congruent to ΔOQT: OT is common.

$\angle OPT = \angle OQT$ (right angles)

$OP = OQ = 5$

So the triangles are congruent.

c. To find the length of *PT*, use ΔOPT noting that the angle *TOP* is one half of the angle found in part **a**, i.e. 0.9 radians:

$$\tan(0.9) = \frac{PT}{5}$$
$$PT = 5\tan(0.9) \text{ (angle in radians)}.$$
$$= 6.3007...$$

So the length of *PT* is 6.3 cm, correct to one decimal place.

d. The area of parallelogram *OPTQ* is $5 \times 6.3 = 31.5$ cm², correct to one decimal place.

The area A of the sector *OPQ* is given by $A = \frac{1}{2}r^2\theta$, where from part **a**, $\theta = 1.8$.

Thus $A = \frac{1.8 \times 5^2}{2} = 22.5$ (cm²).

The area of the shaded region, correct to one decimal place, is $31.5 - 22.5 = 9.0$ (cm²).

Question 136

The angle at Q lies between the sides *PQ* and *QR*. Applying the cosine rule:

$$x^2 + 8^2 - 2 \times x \times 8\cos(60°) = 13^2$$
$$x^2 + 64 - 16x \times \frac{1}{2} = 169$$
$$x^2 - 8x - 105 = 0$$
$$(x+7)(x-15) = 0$$
$$x = 15 \text{ since } x > 0$$

So *QR* has length 15 cm.

Question 137

Now $\angle = 70°$, which is the largest angle, so the longest side will be *AB*.

With the usual labelling convention, the sine rule gives:

$$\frac{a}{\sin(50°)} = \frac{b}{\sin(60°)} = \frac{c}{\sin(70°)}$$

The aim is to find $AB = c$, so express a and b in terms of c:

$$a = \frac{c\sin(50°)}{\sin(70°)} \text{ and } b = \frac{c\sin(60°)}{\sin(70°)}$$

Now $a + b + c = 30$, so:

$$\frac{c\sin(50°)}{\sin(70°)} + \frac{c\sin(60°)}{\sin(70°)} + c = 30$$

$$c = \frac{30\sin(70°)}{\sin(50°) + \sin(60°) + \sin(70°)} = 10.961...$$

$AB = 10.96$ (cm), correct to two decimal places.

Question 138

a. Consider triangle *BCE*.

Let θ be the angle between *BE* and the plane *ABCD*.

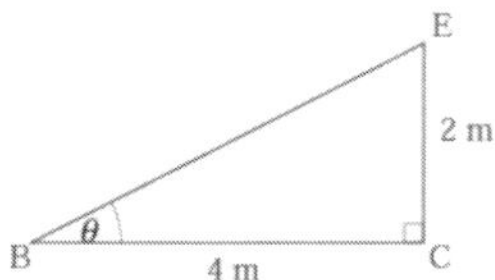

$$\tan(\theta) = \frac{2}{4}$$
$$\theta = 26.6° \text{ (correct to one decimal place)}$$

b. The required angle, denoted by α, can be found from triangle *BDF* because *BD* is directly below *BF*.

The length *BD* can be found by considering the base of the wedge.

$$BD^2 = 4^2 + 5^2$$
$$= 41$$

$$BD = \sqrt{41} \text{ (m)}$$

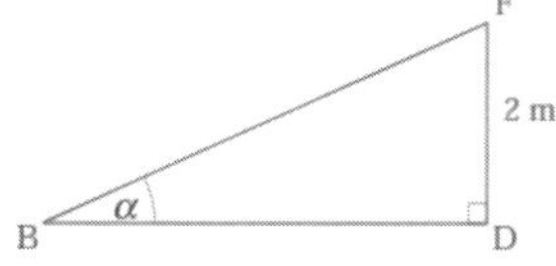

$$\tan(\alpha) = \frac{2}{\sqrt{41}}$$
$$\alpha = 17.3° \text{ (correct to one decimal place)}$$

c. The angle between the planes *ABCD* and *ABEF* is the same as $\angle CBE$.

The angle is 26.6° from part **a**.

d. Consider the triangle BDE with $BD=\sqrt{41}$.

$$BE^2=4^2+2^2$$
$$=20$$

$$BE=\sqrt{20}\text{ (m)}$$

$$DE^2=5^2+2^2$$
$$=29$$

$$DE=\sqrt{29}\text{ (m)}$$

Let β be the angle between BD and BE.

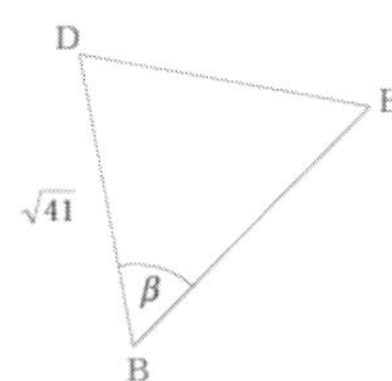

Using the cosine rule:

$$\cos(\beta)=\frac{(\sqrt{41})^2+(\sqrt{20})^2-(\sqrt{29})^2}{2\times\sqrt{41}\times\sqrt{20}}$$
$\beta=56.0°$ (correct to one decimal place)

Question 139

a. This question requires consideration of the ambiguous case of the sine rule.

The two possible answers for angle AQP can be found using the sine rule.

$$\frac{10.4}{\sin(23.5°)}=\frac{20.7}{\sin(Q)}$$

Solving this equation (ensuring that only solutions between 0° and 180° are considered), gives the answers:

$Q=52.5°$ or $127.5°$ $(180°-52.5°)$ (correct to one decimal place)

b. This 'ambiguity' is best understood by viewing an appropriate diagram.

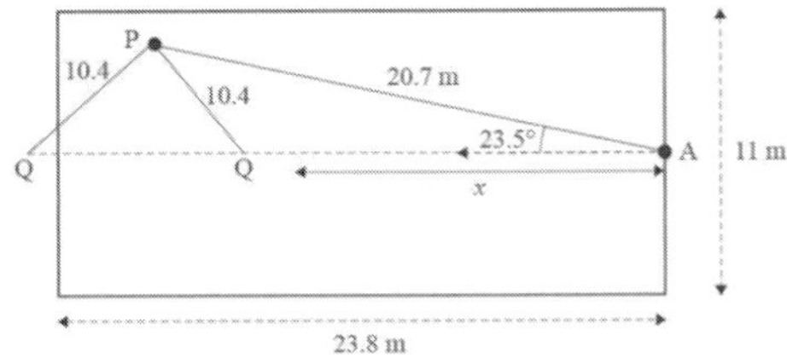

In the diagram above, the angle APQ can be found using:

$$\angle APQ=180°-(23.5°+127.5°)$$
$$=29°$$

The value of x can be found using the sine rule again:

$$\frac{x}{\sin(29°)}=\frac{20.7}{\sin(127.5°)}$$

Solving this equation gives $x=12.65$
which is $x=13$ (m) correct to the nearest metre.

Question 140

a. Factorise $\cos^4(\theta)-\sin^4(\theta)$ and use the Pythagorean identity.

$$\cos^4(\theta)-\sin^4(\theta)$$
$$=(\cos^2(\theta)-\sin^2(\theta))(\cos^2(\theta)+\sin^2(\theta))$$
$$=(\cos^2(\theta)-\sin^2(\theta))(1)$$
$$=\cos^2(\theta)-\sin^2(\theta)$$
$$=\cos(2\theta)$$

b. Use $\sin(2\theta)=2\sin(\theta)\cos(\theta)$ and the Pythagorean identity.

$$\frac{\sin(2\theta)}{1-\cos^2(\theta)}=\frac{\sin(2\theta)}{\sin^2(\theta)}$$
$$=\frac{2\sin(\theta)\cos(\theta)}{\sin^2(\theta)}$$
$$=\frac{2\cos(\theta)}{\sin(\theta)}$$
$$=2\cot(\theta)$$

c. Use $\sin(2\theta)=2\sin(\theta)\cos(\theta)$.

$$\sin(45°)\cos(45°)$$
$$=\frac{1}{2}(2\sin(45°)\cos(45°))$$
$$=\frac{1}{2}\sin(2(45°))$$
$$=\frac{1}{2}\sin(90°)$$
$$=\frac{1}{2}$$

(Alternatively, substitute values directly.)

Question 141

$$\cos(15°)=\cos(45°-30°)$$
$$=\cos(45°)\cos(30°)+\sin(45°)\sin(30°)$$
$$=\frac{\sqrt{2}}{2}\times\frac{\sqrt{3}}{2}+\frac{\sqrt{2}}{2}\times\frac{1}{2}$$
$$=\frac{\sqrt{6}+\sqrt{2}}{4}$$

Question 142

a. To prove $\cos(2\theta)+2\sin^2(\theta)=1$.

$$\text{LHS}=\cos(2\theta)+2\sin^2(\theta)$$
$$=1-2\sin^2(\theta)+2\sin^2(\theta)$$
$$=1$$
$$=\text{RHS}$$

b. To prove $\tan\left(\theta+\frac{\pi}{4}\right)=\frac{1+\tan(\theta)}{1-\tan(\theta)}$.

$$\begin{aligned}\text{LHS}&=\tan\left(\theta+\frac{\pi}{4}\right)\\&=\frac{\tan(\theta)+\tan\left(\frac{\pi}{4}\right)}{1-\tan(\theta)\tan\left(\frac{\pi}{4}\right)}\\&=\frac{\tan(\theta)+1}{1-\tan(\theta)\times 1}\\&=\frac{\tan(\theta)+1}{1-\tan(\theta)}\\&=\frac{1+\tan(\theta)}{1-\tan(\theta)}\\&=\text{RHS}\end{aligned}$$

c. To prove $2\sin\left(\theta-\frac{\pi}{6}\right)=\sqrt{3}\sin(\theta)-\cos(\theta)$.

$$\begin{aligned}\text{LHS}&=2\sin\left(\theta-\frac{\pi}{6}\right)\\&=2\left(\sin(\theta)\cos\left(\frac{\pi}{6}\right)-\cos(\theta)\sin\left(\frac{\pi}{6}\right)\right)\\&=2\left(\sin(\theta)\times\frac{\sqrt{3}}{2}-\cos(\theta)\times\frac{1}{2}\right)\\&=\sqrt{3}\sin(\theta)-\cos(\theta)\times 1\\&=\sqrt{3}\sin(\theta)-\cos(\theta)\\&=\text{RHS}\end{aligned}$$

d. To prove $\sin(3\theta)=3\sin(\theta)-4\sin^3(\theta)$.

$$\begin{aligned}\text{LHS}&=\sin(3\theta)\\&=\sin(\theta+2\theta)\\&=\sin(\theta)\cos(2\theta)+\cos(\theta)\sin(2\theta)\\&=\sin(\theta)\left(1-2\sin^2(\theta)\right)+\cos(\theta)\left(2\sin(\theta)\cos(\theta)\right)\\&=\sin(\theta)-2\sin^3(\theta)+2\cos^2(\theta)\sin(\theta)\\&=\sin(\theta)-2\sin^3(\theta)+2\left(1-\sin^2(\theta)\right)\sin(\theta)\\&=\sin(\theta)-2\sin^3(\theta)+2\sin(\theta)-2\sin^3(\theta)\\&=3\sin(\theta)-4\sin^3(\theta)\\&=\text{RHS}\end{aligned}$$

Question 143

a. Divide $\sin^2(\theta)+\cos^2(\theta)=1$ by $\sin^2(\theta)$ provided $\sin^2(\theta)\neq 0$.

$$\frac{\sin^2(\theta)}{\sin^2(\theta)}+\frac{\cos^2(\theta)}{\sin^2(\theta)}=\frac{1}{\sin^2(\theta)}$$

$$1+\cot^2(\theta)=\operatorname{cosec}^2(\theta)\Rightarrow\operatorname{cosec}^2(\theta)-\cot^2(\theta)=1$$

b. Factor $\operatorname{cosec}^4(\theta)-\cot^4(\theta)$.

$$\begin{aligned}&\operatorname{cosec}^4(\theta)-\cot^4(\theta)\\&=\left(\operatorname{cosec}^2(\theta)-\cot^2(\theta)\right)\left(\operatorname{cosec}^2(\theta)+\cot^2(\theta)\right)\end{aligned}$$

From part (a), $\operatorname{cosec}^2(\theta)-\cot^2(\theta)=1$.

Hence $\operatorname{cosec}^4(\theta)-\cot^4(\theta)=\operatorname{cosec}^2(\theta)+\cot^2(\theta)$.

c. Use parts (a) and (b) to form a quadratic in $\cot(\theta)$.

$$\begin{aligned}1+\cot^2(\theta)+\cot^2(\theta)&=2-\cot(\theta)\\2\cot^2(\theta)+\cot(\theta)-1&=0\\\left(2\cot(\theta)-1\right)\left(\cot(\theta)+1\right)&=0\end{aligned}$$

So $\cot(\theta)=\frac{1}{2}$ or $\cot(\theta)=-1$.

As $\cot(\theta)<0$ in the 2nd quadrant, $\cot(\theta)=-1$

and so $\theta=\frac{3\pi}{4}$.

Question 144

a. Find the values of r and α.

Let $4\sin(\theta)+3\cos(\theta)=r\cos(\theta-\alpha)$.

$=r\cos(\theta)\cos(\alpha)+r\sin(\theta)\sin(\alpha)$

Equating coefficients of $\sin(\theta)$ and $\cos(\theta)$:

$r\sin(\alpha)=4$ (1)

$r\cos(\alpha)=3$ (2)

Squaring (1) and (2) and adding:

$$\begin{aligned}r^2\left(\sin^2(\alpha)+\cos^2(\alpha)\right)&=4^2+3^2\\r^2&=25\end{aligned}$$

So $r=5$ (as $r>0$).

From (1) and (2):

$\sin(\alpha)=\frac{4}{5}$ and $\cos(\alpha)=\frac{3}{5}$

So $\tan\alpha=\frac{4}{3}$ and $\alpha=\tan^{-1}\left(\frac{4}{3}\right)$.

Hence $4\sin(\theta)+3\cos(\theta)$ can be expressed as

$5\cos\left(\theta-\tan^{-1}\left(\frac{4}{3}\right)\right)$.

b. The maximum value of $\cos\left(\theta-\tan^{-1}\left(\frac{4}{3}\right)\right)$ is 1.

The maximum value of $5\cos\left(\theta-\tan^{-1}\left(\frac{4}{3}\right)\right)$ is 5.

So the maximum value of $4\sin(\theta)+3\cos(\theta)$ is 5.

$\cos\left(\theta-\tan^{-1}\left(\frac{4}{3}\right)\right)=1$ when $\theta-\tan^{-1}\left(\frac{4}{3}\right)=0$

Hence $\theta=\tan^{-1}\left(\frac{4}{3}\right)$.

c. Using part (a), $T = 5\cos\left(\frac{\pi}{12}t - \tan^{-1}\left(\frac{4}{3}\right)\right) + 15$.

The minimum temperature occurs when

$$\cos\left(\frac{\pi}{12}t - \tan^{-1}\left(\frac{4}{3}\right)\right) = -1.$$

The minimum temperature is $(-5+15)°\text{C} = 10°\text{C}$.

d. $\cos\left(\frac{\pi}{12}t - \tan^{-1}\left(\frac{4}{3}\right)\right) = \cos(\pi)$

$$\begin{aligned}\frac{\pi}{12}t - \tan^{-1}\left(\frac{4}{3}\right) &= \pi \\ \frac{\pi}{12}t &= \pi + \tan^{-1}\left(\frac{4}{3}\right) \\ t &= \frac{12}{\pi}\left(\pi + \tan^{-1}\left(\frac{4}{3}\right)\right) \\ &= 15.5420\ldots \text{ (hours)}\end{aligned}$$

The minimum temperature occurs when $t = 15.5$ (hours) (correct to 1 decimal place).

Question 145

a. $\text{LHS} = 2\sin(x)\left(\cos(2x) + \cos(4x) + \cos(6x)\right)$

$$\begin{aligned}&= 2\cos(2x)\sin(x) + 2\cos(4x)\sin(x) + 2\cos(6x)\sin(x) \\ &= \sin(2x+x) - \sin(2x-x) + \sin(4x+x) - \sin(4x-x) \\ &\quad + \sin(6x+x) - \sin(6x-x) \\ &= \sin(3x) - \sin(x) + \sin(5x) - \sin(3x) + \sin(7x) - \sin(5x) \\ &= \sin(7x) - \sin(x) \\ &= \text{RHS}\end{aligned}$$

b. Let $x = \frac{\pi}{7}$.

$$\begin{aligned}&2\sin\left(\frac{\pi}{7}\right)\left(\cos\left(\frac{2\pi}{7}\right) + \cos\left(\frac{4\pi}{7}\right) + \cos\left(\frac{6\pi}{7}\right)\right) \\ &= \sin(\pi) - \sin\left(\frac{\pi}{7}\right)\end{aligned}$$

$$\begin{aligned}\cos\left(\frac{2\pi}{7}\right) + \cos\left(\frac{4\pi}{7}\right) + \cos\left(\frac{6\pi}{7}\right) &= \frac{\sin(\pi) - \sin\left(\frac{\pi}{7}\right)}{2\sin\left(\frac{\pi}{7}\right)} \\ &= -\frac{1}{2}\end{aligned}$$

c. Use $\cos(\pi - \theta) = -\cos(\theta) \Rightarrow \cos(\theta) = -\cos(\pi - \theta)$.

$$\begin{aligned}&\cos\left(\frac{2\pi}{7}\right) + \cos\left(\frac{4\pi}{7}\right) + \cos\left(\frac{6\pi}{7}\right) \\ &= -\cos\left(\pi - \frac{2\pi}{7}\right) - \cos\left(\pi - \frac{4\pi}{7}\right) - \cos\left(\pi - \frac{6\pi}{7}\right) \\ &= -\cos\left(\frac{5\pi}{7}\right) - \cos\left(\frac{3\pi}{7}\right) - \cos\left(\frac{\pi}{7}\right)\end{aligned}$$

$$\begin{aligned}-\left(\cos\left(\frac{5\pi}{7}\right) + \cos\left(\frac{3\pi}{7}\right) + \cos\left(\frac{\pi}{7}\right)\right) &= -\left(-\frac{1}{2}\right) \\ &= \frac{1}{2}\end{aligned}$$

So $\cos\left(\frac{\pi}{7}\right) + \cos\left(\frac{3\pi}{7}\right) + \cos\left(\frac{5\pi}{7}\right) = \frac{1}{2}$.

Solutions: B3

Question 146 D

The matrix of translation can be represented as

$\begin{bmatrix} x \\ y \end{bmatrix}$, and so $\begin{bmatrix} \sqrt{3} \\ -\sqrt{2} \end{bmatrix} + \begin{bmatrix} x \\ y \end{bmatrix} = \begin{bmatrix} -\sqrt{3} \\ -\sqrt{2} \end{bmatrix}$.

So $x = -2\sqrt{3}$ and $y = 0$.

Question 147 A

From the common trigonometric values in the given matrix, it appears to be a rotation matrix, which has the form

$\begin{bmatrix} \cos(\theta) & -\sin(\theta) \\ \sin(\theta) & \cos(\theta) \end{bmatrix}$.

Checking the values:

$$\cos(\theta) = \frac{\sqrt{3}}{2} \text{ and } \sin(\theta) = \frac{1}{2} \Leftrightarrow \theta = 30^\circ$$

So the matrix represents a rotation (anticlockwise) of 30° about the origin.

Question 148 C

Apply the transformation:

$$\begin{aligned} \begin{bmatrix} x' \\ y' \end{bmatrix} &= \begin{bmatrix} \frac{1}{2} & -\frac{\sqrt{3}}{2} \\ \frac{\sqrt{3}}{2} & \frac{1}{2} \end{bmatrix} \begin{bmatrix} 2 \\ 0 \end{bmatrix} \\ &= \begin{bmatrix} 1 \\ \sqrt{3} \end{bmatrix} \end{aligned}$$

Question 149 C

The transformation is a shear parallel to the x-axis by a factor of 3, which is represented by

the matrix $\begin{bmatrix} 1 & 3 \\ 0 & 1 \end{bmatrix}$.

Question 150 B

The graph of S is a 270° anticlockwise rotation of the graph of R, and so the rotation matrix is

$$\begin{aligned} T &= \begin{bmatrix} \cos(\theta) & -\sin(\theta) \\ \sin(\theta) & \cos(\theta) \end{bmatrix} \\ &= \begin{bmatrix} \cos(270^\circ) & -\sin(270^\circ) \\ \sin(270^\circ) & \cos(270^\circ) \end{bmatrix} \\ &= \begin{bmatrix} 0 & 1 \\ -1 & 0 \end{bmatrix} \end{aligned}$$

Question 151 D

Applying the dilation and then the translation, the image point can be found as follows:

$$\begin{aligned} \begin{bmatrix} x' \\ y' \end{bmatrix} &= \begin{bmatrix} 1 & 0 \\ 0 & 3 \end{bmatrix} \begin{bmatrix} -1 \\ 2 \end{bmatrix} + \begin{bmatrix} 2 \\ 1 \end{bmatrix} \\ &= \begin{bmatrix} 1 \\ 7 \end{bmatrix} \end{aligned}$$

Question 152 A

A 90° anticlockwise rotation can be represented by the matrix

$$\begin{aligned} T &= \begin{bmatrix} \cos(\theta) & -\sin(\theta) \\ \sin(\theta) & \cos(\theta) \end{bmatrix} \\ &= \begin{bmatrix} \cos(90^\circ) & -\sin(90^\circ) \\ \sin(90^\circ) & \cos(90^\circ) \end{bmatrix} \\ &= \begin{bmatrix} 0 & -1 \\ 1 & 0 \end{bmatrix} \end{aligned}$$

Question 153 D

The area of the given rectangle is $3 \times 2 = 6$.

The determinant of the transformation matrix is

$$\begin{aligned} \det &= ad - bc \\ &= 1 \times 1 - (-1 \times 1) \\ &= 2 \end{aligned}$$

So the area of the image is $6 \times 2 = 12$.

Question 154 B

The matrix for a dilation by a factor of 2 parallel to the x-axis is $\begin{bmatrix} 2 & 0 \\ 0 & 1 \end{bmatrix}$. So

$$\begin{aligned} \begin{bmatrix} x' \\ y' \end{bmatrix} &= \begin{bmatrix} 2 & 0 \\ 0 & 1 \end{bmatrix} \begin{bmatrix} x \\ y \end{bmatrix} \\ &= \begin{bmatrix} 2x \\ y \end{bmatrix} \end{aligned}$$

Under this transformation:

$$x' = 2x \Leftrightarrow x = \frac{x'}{2}$$

$$y' = y \Leftrightarrow y = y'$$

The equation $y = 2x + 1$ becomes:

$$y' = 2\left(\frac{x'}{2}\right) + 1$$

$$y' = x' + 1$$

The equation of the image is $y = x + 1$.

Question 155 D

The area has changed from 1 to 9 square units.

The matrix of transformation is $T = \begin{bmatrix} 3 & 0 \\ 0 & 3 \end{bmatrix}$,

which is a dilation in both x and y directions by a factor of 3.

The determinant of T is

$$\begin{aligned}\det T &= ad - bc \\ &= 3\times 3 - 0\times 0 \\ &= 9\end{aligned}$$

Question 156 B

The matrix for reflection in the x-axis is

$A = \begin{bmatrix} 1 & 0 \\ 0 & -1 \end{bmatrix}$ and the rotation matrix is

$B = \frac{1}{2}\begin{bmatrix} 1 & -\sqrt{3} \\ \sqrt{3} & 1 \end{bmatrix}$.

The product matrix BA represents the effect of A followed by B, i.e. it will give the matrix of the composite transformation.

Question 157

a. This is a translation to the right by 1 unit and down by 2 units.

The equation of the image is $y = (x-1)^2 - 2$.

b. This is a dilation by a factor of 4 from the x-axis (i.e. parallel to the y-axis).

The equation of the image is $y = 4x^2$.

c. This is a reflection in the x-axis.

The equation of the image is $y = -x^2$.

d. $\begin{bmatrix} x' \\ y' \end{bmatrix} = \begin{bmatrix} 0 & 1 \\ -1 & 0 \end{bmatrix}\begin{bmatrix} x \\ y \end{bmatrix} = \begin{bmatrix} y \\ -x \end{bmatrix}$

So $y = x'$ and $x = -y'$.

The equation $y = x^2$ becomes $x' = (-y')^2$.

The equation of the image is $x = y^2$.

This parabola is the inverse graph of the given parabola $(y = x^2)$.

As a transformation, the effect is to reflect the graph of $y = x^2$ in the line $y = x$.

However, note that

$\begin{bmatrix} 0 & 1 \\ -1 & 0 \end{bmatrix} = \begin{bmatrix} 1 & 0 \\ 0 & -1 \end{bmatrix}\begin{bmatrix} 0 & 1 \\ 1 & 0 \end{bmatrix}$, so the transformation is actually a reflection in the line $y = x$ followed by a reflection in the x-axis, but this latter reflection has no discernible effect.

Question 158

a. $A = \begin{bmatrix} -\frac{3}{5} & -\frac{4}{5} \\ -\frac{4}{5} & \frac{3}{5} \end{bmatrix}$ and $\det A = -1$.

A has the form $\begin{bmatrix} a & b \\ b & -a \end{bmatrix}$.

So A is a reflection matrix where

$\cos(2\theta) = -\frac{3}{5}$ and $\sin(2\theta) = -\frac{4}{5}$.

Hence $\tan(2\theta) = \frac{4}{3}$, where $-\pi < 2\theta < 0$.

If $m = \tan(\theta)$ and $\tan(2\theta) = \frac{2\tan(\theta)}{1-\tan^2(\theta)}$,

$\frac{2m}{1-m^2} = \frac{4}{3}$.

$$\begin{aligned}2m^2 + 3m - 2 &= 0 \\ (2m-1)(m+2) &= 0 \\ m &= \frac{1}{2}, -2\end{aligned}$$

As $-\frac{\pi}{2} < \theta < 0$, then $m < 0$.

So $\tan(\theta) = -2$.

The transformation is a reflection in the line $y = -2x$.

b. $A = \begin{bmatrix} \frac{3}{5} & -\frac{4}{5} \\ \frac{4}{5} & \frac{3}{5} \end{bmatrix}$ and $\det A = 1$.

A has the form $\begin{bmatrix} a & -b \\ b & a \end{bmatrix}$.

So A is a rotation matrix (anticlockwise about O).

Let the angle of rotation be α.

So $\cos(\alpha) = \frac{3}{5}$ and $\sin(\alpha) = \frac{4}{5}$.

Hence $\tan(\alpha) = \frac{4}{3} \Rightarrow \alpha = \tan^{-1}\left(\frac{4}{3}\right)$.

The transformation is an anticlockwise rotation about $O(0,0)$ through $\tan^{-1}\left(\frac{4}{3}\right)$.

Question 159

Let T_1 represent the reflection in the line $y=-x$.

As $m=\tan(\theta)$, $\tan(\theta)=-1 \Rightarrow \theta=\frac{3\pi}{4}$

(where θ is the angle between the positive direction of the x-axis and the line $y=-x$).

T_1 has matrix:

$$A=\begin{bmatrix}\cos\left(\frac{3\pi}{2}\right) & \sin\left(\frac{3\pi}{2}\right)\\ \sin\left(\frac{3\pi}{2}\right) & -\cos\left(\frac{3\pi}{2}\right)\end{bmatrix}=\begin{bmatrix}0 & -1\\ -1 & 0\end{bmatrix}.$$

Let T_2 represent by an anticlockwise rotation of $\frac{3\pi}{4}$ about O.

T_2 has matrix:

$$B=\begin{bmatrix}\cos\left(\frac{3\pi}{4}\right) & -\sin\left(\frac{3\pi}{4}\right)\\ \sin\left(\frac{3\pi}{4}\right) & \cos\left(\frac{3\pi}{4}\right)\end{bmatrix}=\begin{bmatrix}-\frac{1}{\sqrt{2}} & -\frac{1}{\sqrt{2}}\\ \frac{1}{\sqrt{2}} & -\frac{1}{\sqrt{2}}\end{bmatrix}.$$

The matrix of the combined transformation, BA is:

$$BA=\begin{bmatrix}-\frac{1}{\sqrt{2}} & -\frac{1}{\sqrt{2}}\\ \frac{1}{\sqrt{2}} & -\frac{1}{\sqrt{2}}\end{bmatrix}\begin{bmatrix}0 & -1\\ -1 & 0\end{bmatrix}=\begin{bmatrix}\frac{1}{\sqrt{2}} & \frac{1}{\sqrt{2}}\\ \frac{1}{\sqrt{2}} & -\frac{1}{\sqrt{2}}\end{bmatrix}$$

If (x',y') are the coordinates of the image of (x,y), then:

$$\begin{bmatrix}x'\\ y'\end{bmatrix}=\begin{bmatrix}\frac{1}{\sqrt{2}} & \frac{1}{\sqrt{2}}\\ \frac{1}{\sqrt{2}} & -\frac{1}{\sqrt{2}}\end{bmatrix}\begin{bmatrix}x\\ y\end{bmatrix}=\begin{bmatrix}\frac{1}{\sqrt{2}}(x+y)\\ \frac{1}{\sqrt{2}}(x-y)\end{bmatrix}$$

So $x'=\frac{1}{\sqrt{2}}(x+y)$ and $y'=\frac{1}{\sqrt{2}}(x-y)$.

Solving for x and y gives:

$x=\frac{1}{\sqrt{2}}(x'+y')$ and $y=\frac{1}{\sqrt{2}}(x'-y')$

The equation $y=2x-1$ becomes:

$$\frac{1}{\sqrt{2}}(x'-y')=2\left(\frac{1}{\sqrt{2}}(x'+y')\right)-1$$
$$x'-y'=2x'+2y'-\sqrt{2}$$
$$x'+3y'-\sqrt{2}=0$$

The equation of the image is $x+3y=\sqrt{2}$.

Question 160

a. $M=\begin{bmatrix}4 & -1\\ 3 & 1\end{bmatrix}$ and $\det M=7$.

$$M^{-1}=\frac{1}{7}\begin{bmatrix}1 & 1\\ -3 & 4\end{bmatrix}$$

$$MX=B$$
$$M^{-1}MX=M^{-1}B$$
$$X=M^{-1}B$$

Let the vertices of T_1 be P_1, Q_1 and R_1 respectively.

Coordinates of P_1:

$$\frac{1}{7}\begin{bmatrix}1 & 1\\ -3 & 4\end{bmatrix}\begin{bmatrix}4\\ 3\end{bmatrix}=\begin{bmatrix}1\\ 0\end{bmatrix}$$

So $P_1(1,0)$.

Coordinates of Q_1:

$$\frac{1}{7}\begin{bmatrix}1 & 1\\ -3 & 4\end{bmatrix}\begin{bmatrix}4\\ 10\end{bmatrix}=\begin{bmatrix}2\\ 4\end{bmatrix}$$

So $Q_1(2,4)$.

Coordinates of R_1:

$$\frac{1}{7}\begin{bmatrix}1 & 1\\ -3 & 4\end{bmatrix}\begin{bmatrix}16\\ 12\end{bmatrix}=\begin{bmatrix}4\\ 0\end{bmatrix}$$

So $R_1(4,0)$.

b. The area of T_1 is $\frac{1}{2}\times 3\times 4=6$ (sq. units).

c. From part (a), $\det M=7$.

Hence the area of T_2 is $6\times 7=42$ (sq. units).

Solutions: B4

Question 161 C

$$3\underset{\sim}{a}-\underset{\sim}{b}=3\begin{bmatrix}1\\-2\end{bmatrix}-\begin{bmatrix}-3\\1\end{bmatrix}=\begin{bmatrix}3\\-6\end{bmatrix}-\begin{bmatrix}-3\\1\end{bmatrix}=\begin{bmatrix}6\\-7\end{bmatrix}$$

Question 162 E

$$\begin{aligned}\overrightarrow{AB}&=\overrightarrow{AO}+\overrightarrow{OB}\\&=-\overrightarrow{OA}+\overrightarrow{OB}\\&=-(3\underset{\sim}{i}-\underset{\sim}{j})+(-\underset{\sim}{i}+2\underset{\sim}{j})\\&=-4\underset{\sim}{i}+3\underset{\sim}{j}\end{aligned}$$

Question 163 C

$$|3\underset{\sim}{i}-2\underset{\sim}{j}|=\sqrt{3^2+(-2)^2}=\sqrt{13}$$

So a unit vector in the direction of the given vector is $\frac{1}{\sqrt{13}}(3\underset{\sim}{i}-2\underset{\sim}{j})$.

(Note that **E** is a unit vector in the opposite direction.)

Question 164 C

The expression 'position vectors' means that the vectors start at the origin O.

$$\begin{aligned}\overrightarrow{PQ}&=\overrightarrow{PO}+\overrightarrow{OQ}\\&=-\overrightarrow{OP}+\overrightarrow{OQ}\\&=-\underset{\sim}{p}+\underset{\sim}{q}\end{aligned}$$

If P, Q and R lie in a straight line, then this must be parallel to the vector from Q to R, which is $3\underset{\sim}{i}+\underset{\sim}{j}$.

Now alternative **C** can be written as $-\underset{\sim}{p}+\underset{\sim}{q}=2(3\underset{\sim}{i}+\underset{\sim}{j})$ and this means that the vector $-\underset{\sim}{p}+\underset{\sim}{q}$ is twice the magnitude of the vector from Q to R and in the same direction as the vector from Q to R.

Question 165 D

In **D**, the vectors are certainly unit vectors and $\left(\frac{1}{\sqrt{2}}\underset{\sim}{i}-\frac{1}{\sqrt{2}}\underset{\sim}{j}\right)\cdot\left(\frac{1}{\sqrt{2}}\underset{\sim}{i}+\frac{1}{\sqrt{2}}\underset{\sim}{j}\right)=\frac{1}{2}-\frac{1}{2}=0$, so they are also perpendicular.

A and **B** cannot be true as the vectors are not unit vectors.

E is not true since the second vector is not a unit vector.

C is not true since $\left(\frac{1}{\sqrt{2}}\underset{\sim}{i}-\frac{1}{\sqrt{2}}\underset{\sim}{j}\right)\cdot\left(-\frac{1}{\sqrt{2}}\underset{\sim}{i}+\frac{1}{\sqrt{2}}\underset{\sim}{j}\right)=-1$, so these vectors are not perpendicular.

Question 166 E

The vector resolute is given by $(\underset{\sim}{a}\cdot\hat{\underset{\sim}{b}})\hat{\underset{\sim}{b}}$.

The scalar resolute is given by $\underset{\sim}{a}\cdot\hat{\underset{\sim}{b}}$.

Given $\underset{\sim}{a}\cdot\hat{\underset{\sim}{b}}=-4$ and $\underset{\sim}{b}=-\sqrt{3}\underset{\sim}{i}$, then $\hat{\underset{\sim}{b}}=-\underset{\sim}{i}$ and the vector resolute is $(-4)(-\underset{\sim}{i})=4\underset{\sim}{i}$.

Question 167 D

$$\cos(\theta)=\frac{\underset{\sim}{a}\cdot\underset{\sim}{b}}{|\underset{\sim}{a}||\underset{\sim}{b}|}=\frac{x-1}{\sqrt{2}\sqrt{x^2+1}}$$

$$\cos(\phi)=\frac{\underset{\sim}{b}\cdot\underset{\sim}{c}}{|\underset{\sim}{b}||\underset{\sim}{c}|}=\frac{1-x}{\sqrt{2}\sqrt{1+x^2}}$$

$$\cos(\theta)\cos(\phi)=\frac{(x-1)(1-x)}{2(1+x^2)}=-\frac{(x-1)^2}{2(1+x^2)}$$

(The expression for $\cos(\theta)\cos(\phi)$ can be found directly using the vector features of a CAS.)

Question 168 A

The vectors $\underset{\sim}{a},\underset{\sim}{b}$ and $\underset{\sim}{a}+\underset{\sim}{b}$ form a triangle.

The sum of the lengths of any two sides of a triangle is greater than the length of the third side except in the 'degenerate' case where two of the sides lie in a straight line along the third side.

Thus for the vectors given $|\underset{\sim}{a}+\underset{\sim}{b}|\le|\underset{\sim}{a}|+|\underset{\sim}{b}|$ with equality only if $\underset{\sim}{a}$ and $\underset{\sim}{b}$ are in the same direction, i.e. if they are parallel.

(Note that alternative **A** correctly states that it is **necessary** that the vectors are parallel.

Alternative **C** is a special case of this but it does not follow necessarily from the original statement.)

Question 169 B

Change in displacement is given by

$$\underset{\sim}{s}_f - \underset{\sim}{s}_i = (-\underset{\sim}{i} + 5\underset{\sim}{j}) - (3\underset{\sim}{i} + \underset{\sim}{j}) = -4\underset{\sim}{i} + 4\underset{\sim}{j}$$

This change occurs over 2 seconds, so the constant velocity is given by

$$\underset{\sim}{v} = \frac{-4\underset{\sim}{i} + 4\underset{\sim}{j}}{2} = -2\underset{\sim}{i} + 2\underset{\sim}{j}$$

Question 170 A

The scalar resolute of the force in the given direction is:

$$\underset{\sim}{F} \cdot \hat{\underset{\sim}{w}} = (a\underset{\sim}{i} + b\underset{\sim}{j}) \cdot \frac{1}{\sqrt{2}}(\underset{\sim}{i} + \underset{\sim}{j})$$
$$= \frac{1}{\sqrt{2}}(a+b)$$

The vector component is:

$$\frac{1}{\sqrt{2}}(a+b)\hat{\underset{\sim}{w}} = \left(\frac{a+b}{\sqrt{2}}\right) \times \frac{1}{\sqrt{2}}\underset{\sim}{w}$$
$$= \left(\frac{a+b}{2}\right)\underset{\sim}{w}$$

Question 171 B

Here is a sketch showing the two forces $\underset{\sim}{A}$ and $\underset{\sim}{B}$.

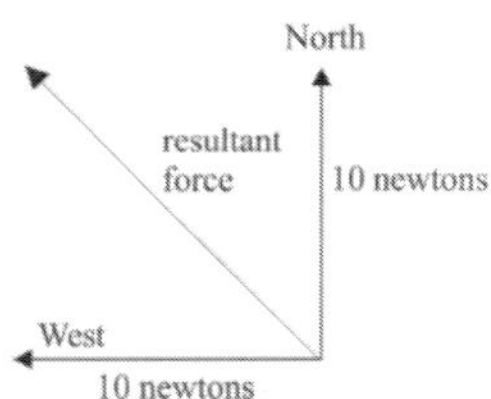

The resultant force has magnitude $\sqrt{10^2 + 10^2} = \sqrt{200} = 10\sqrt{2}$.

It acts in a direction exactly northwest (by symmetry).

As the particle is stationary, $\underset{\sim}{C}$ must be equal in magnitude and opposite in direction to this resultant force.

Thus force $\underset{\sim}{C}$ has magnitude $10\sqrt{2}$ newtons and direction southeast.

Question 172 A

Direction of F_1:

$$F_1 + 6\cos(30°) = F_2\cos(60°) + 8$$
$$F_1 = \frac{1}{2}F_2 + 8 - 3\sqrt{3} \qquad (*)$$

Direction perpendicular to F_1:

$$F_2 \sin(60°) = 6\sin(30°)$$
$$\frac{\sqrt{3}}{2}F_2 = 6 \times \frac{1}{2}$$
$$F_2 = \frac{6}{\sqrt{3}}$$
$$= 2\sqrt{3}$$

Substituting in $(*)$:

$$F_1 = \sqrt{3} + 8 - 3\sqrt{3}$$
$$= 8 - 2\sqrt{3}$$

(A CAS could be used to solve simultaneously for F_1 and F_2.)

Question 173

Let $\overrightarrow{MC} = \underset{\sim}{a}$ and $\overrightarrow{NC} = \underset{\sim}{b}$.

So $\overrightarrow{MN} = \underset{\sim}{a} - \underset{\sim}{b}$.

Now $\overrightarrow{AC} = 2\underset{\sim}{a}$ and $\overrightarrow{BC} = 2\underset{\sim}{b}$.

So $\overrightarrow{AB} = 2\underset{\sim}{a} - 2\underset{\sim}{b} = 2(\underset{\sim}{a} - \underset{\sim}{b})$.

Hence $\overrightarrow{AB} = 2\overrightarrow{MN}$, i.e. $\overrightarrow{MN} = \frac{1}{2}\overrightarrow{AB}$ and therefore MN is parallel to AB and half its length.

Question 174

a. $\overrightarrow{OC} = \underset{\sim}{a} + \underset{\sim}{b}$

$$\text{LHS} = \overrightarrow{OC} \cdot \overrightarrow{OC}$$
$$= (\underset{\sim}{a} + \underset{\sim}{b}) \cdot (\underset{\sim}{a} + \underset{\sim}{b})$$
$$= \underset{\sim}{a} \cdot \underset{\sim}{a} + \underset{\sim}{a} \cdot \underset{\sim}{b} + \underset{\sim}{b} \cdot \underset{\sim}{a} + \underset{\sim}{b} \cdot \underset{\sim}{b}$$
$$= a^2 + 2\underset{\sim}{a} \cdot \underset{\sim}{b} + b^2$$
$$= \text{RHS}$$

In the above, $\underset{\sim}{a} \cdot \underset{\sim}{a} = a^2$ and $\underset{\sim}{b} \cdot \underset{\sim}{b} = b^2$.

So $\left|\overrightarrow{OC}\right|^2 = a^2 + 2\underset{\sim}{a} \cdot \underset{\sim}{b} + b^2$

b. $\overrightarrow{AB} = \underset{\sim}{b} - \underset{\sim}{a}$

$$\text{LHS} = \overrightarrow{AB} \cdot \overrightarrow{AB}$$
$$= (\underset{\sim}{b} - \underset{\sim}{a}) \cdot (\underset{\sim}{b} - \underset{\sim}{a})$$
$$= \underset{\sim}{b} \cdot \underset{\sim}{b} - \underset{\sim}{b} \cdot \underset{\sim}{a} - \underset{\sim}{a} \cdot \underset{\sim}{b} + \underset{\sim}{a} \cdot \underset{\sim}{a}$$
$$= b^2 - 2\underset{\sim}{a} \cdot \underset{\sim}{b} + a^2$$
$$= \text{RHS}$$

So $\left|\overrightarrow{AB}\right|^2 = b^2 - 2\underset{\sim}{a} \cdot \underset{\sim}{b} + a^2$.

c. $OC = AB \Rightarrow |\overrightarrow{OC}|^2 = |\overrightarrow{AB}|^2$

$$a^2 + 2\underset{\sim}{a}\cdot\underset{\sim}{b} + b^2 = b^2 - 2\underset{\sim}{a}\cdot\underset{\sim}{b} + a^2$$
$$4\underset{\sim}{a}\cdot\underset{\sim}{b} = 0$$

Hence $\underset{\sim}{a}\cdot\underset{\sim}{b} = 0$ and so $OACB$ is a rectangle because it is a parallelogram with adjacent sides at right angles.

Question 175

Using the dot product: $\underset{\sim}{v}\cdot\underset{\sim}{w} = a + a = 2a$.

Also:

$$\begin{aligned}\underset{\sim}{v}\cdot\underset{\sim}{w} &= |\underset{\sim}{v}||\underset{\sim}{w}|\cos(\theta)\\ &= \sqrt{a^2+1}\times\sqrt{a^2+1}\times\cos(30^\circ)\\ &= \frac{\sqrt{3}}{2}(a^2+1)\end{aligned}$$

So $\frac{\sqrt{3}}{2}(a^2+1) = 2a$.

Solving gives:

$$\begin{aligned}\sqrt{3}a^2 + \sqrt{3} &= 4a\\ \sqrt{3}a^2 - 4a + \sqrt{3} &= 0\\ a &= \frac{4\pm\sqrt{16-12}}{2\sqrt{3}}\\ &= \frac{4\pm 2}{2\sqrt{3}}\\ &= \frac{3}{\sqrt{3}} \text{ or } \frac{1}{\sqrt{3}}\end{aligned}$$

So the possible values of a are $\sqrt{3}$ or $\frac{1}{\sqrt{3}}$.

Question 176

Let Kate's first path be described by the vector $\overrightarrow{OA}$ and the second path by the vector $\overrightarrow{AB}$.

Then in component form:

$$\begin{aligned}\overrightarrow{OA} &= 4\cos(45^\circ)\underset{\sim}{i} + 4\sin(45^\circ)\underset{\sim}{j}\\ &= 4\left(\frac{1}{\sqrt{2}}\underset{\sim}{i} + \frac{1}{\sqrt{2}}\underset{\sim}{j}\right)\\ &= 2\sqrt{2}(\underset{\sim}{i}+\underset{\sim}{j})\end{aligned}$$

$$\begin{aligned}\overrightarrow{AB} &= 6\cos(300^\circ)\underset{\sim}{i} + 6\sin(300^\circ)\underset{\sim}{j}\\ &= 6\left(\frac{1}{2}\underset{\sim}{i} - \frac{\sqrt{3}}{2}\underset{\sim}{j}\right)\\ &= 3(\underset{\sim}{i} - \sqrt{3}\underset{\sim}{j})\end{aligned}$$

Kate's final path is described by the vector BO, so:

$$\begin{aligned}\overrightarrow{BO} &= \overrightarrow{BA} + \overrightarrow{AO}\\ &= -\overrightarrow{AB} - \overrightarrow{OA}\\ &= -3(\underset{\sim}{i} - \sqrt{3}\underset{\sim}{j}) - 2\sqrt{2}(\underset{\sim}{i}+\underset{\sim}{j})\\ &= (-3-2\sqrt{2})\underset{\sim}{i} + (3\sqrt{3}-2\sqrt{2})\underset{\sim}{j}\end{aligned}$$

Question 177

Let $\underset{\sim}{v}_B - \underset{\sim}{v}_A$ represent the velocity of B relative to A where $\underset{\sim}{v}_A$ is the velocity of A relative to Earth and $\underset{\sim}{v}_B$ is the velocity of B relative to Earth.

$$\begin{aligned}\underset{\sim}{v}_B - \underset{\sim}{v}_A &= (3\underset{\sim}{i} + 7\underset{\sim}{j}) - (5\underset{\sim}{i} - 4\underset{\sim}{j})\\ &= -2\underset{\sim}{i} + 11\underset{\sim}{j}\end{aligned}$$

The bearing is given by $270^\circ + \theta$ where

$$\theta = \tan^{-1}\left(\frac{11}{2}\right) = 79.69^\circ\ldots$$

So the bearing is 350°.

Question 178

When Cadel is cycling at $u\underset{\sim}{j}$ ms^{-1}:

$$\begin{aligned}c(3\underset{\sim}{i} - 4\underset{\sim}{j}) &= \underset{\sim}{v} - u\underset{\sim}{j}\\ \underset{\sim}{v} &= 3c\underset{\sim}{i} + (u-4c)\underset{\sim}{j} \quad (1)\end{aligned}$$

When Cadel is cycling at $\frac{1}{5}u(-3\underset{\sim}{i} + 4\underset{\sim}{j})$ ms^{-1}:

$$\begin{aligned}k\underset{\sim}{i} &= \underset{\sim}{v} - \frac{u}{5}(-3\underset{\sim}{i} + 4\underset{\sim}{j})\\ \underset{\sim}{v} &= k\underset{\sim}{i} + \frac{u}{5}(-3\underset{\sim}{i} + 4\underset{\sim}{j})\\ &= \left(k - \frac{3u}{5}\right)\underset{\sim}{i} + \frac{4u}{5}\underset{\sim}{j} \quad (2)\end{aligned}$$

Equating the $\underset{\sim}{j}$ components of (1) and (2):

$$u - 4c = \frac{4u}{5} \Rightarrow c = \frac{u}{20}$$

Substituting into (1) gives:

$$\underset{\sim}{v} = \frac{3u}{20}\underset{\sim}{i} + \frac{4u}{5}\underset{\sim}{j}$$

Question 179

a. $\underset{\sim}{F} = (6\underset{\sim}{i} + 2\underset{\sim}{j}) + (3\underset{\sim}{i} - 5\underset{\sim}{j}) = (9\underset{\sim}{i} - 3\underset{\sim}{j})$ N

b. $\cos(\theta) = \dfrac{\underset{\sim}{F} \cdot \underset{\sim}{j}}{|\underset{\sim}{F}||\underset{\sim}{j}|}$

$$\cos(\theta) = \frac{(9\underset{\sim}{i} - 3\underset{\sim}{j}) \cdot \underset{\sim}{j}}{|9\underset{\sim}{i} - 3\underset{\sim}{j}||\underset{\sim}{j}|}$$

$$= -\frac{3}{\sqrt{9^2 + (-3)^2}\sqrt{1}}$$

$$= -\frac{3}{\sqrt{90}}$$

$$\theta = \cos^{-1}\left(-\frac{3}{\sqrt{90}}\right)$$

$$= 108.4°$$

So the angle between $\underset{\sim}{F}$ and $\underset{\sim}{j}$ is $108.4°$, correct to one decimal place.

c. Use $\underset{\sim}{F} = m\underset{\sim}{a}$ with $\underset{\sim}{F} = 9\underset{\sim}{i} - 3\underset{\sim}{j}$ and $m = 3$.

$$9\underset{\sim}{i} - 3\underset{\sim}{j} = 3\underset{\sim}{a}$$

$$\underset{\sim}{a} = 3\underset{\sim}{i} - \underset{\sim}{j}$$

The acceleration of the particle is $(3\underset{\sim}{i} - \underset{\sim}{j})$ ms^{-2}.

d. The velocity of the particle after 2 seconds is $(-2\underset{\sim}{i} + \underset{\sim}{j}) + 2(3\underset{\sim}{i} - \underset{\sim}{j}) = (4\underset{\sim}{i} - \underset{\sim}{j})$ ms^{-1}.

The speed of the particle after 2 seconds is $\sqrt{4^2 + (-1)^2} = \sqrt{17}$ (ms^{-1}).

Question 180

a. As the plane is smooth, the only other forces are a vertical weight of magnitude $10g$ and a normal reaction of magnitude R perpendicular to the plane:

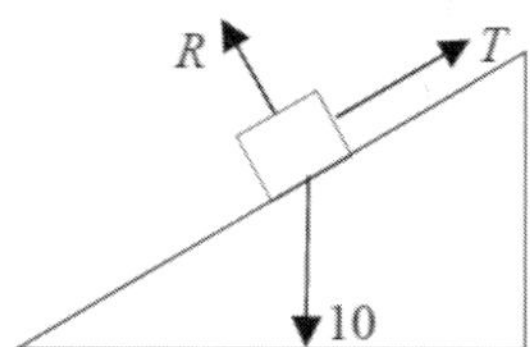

b. Resolving parallel to the plane gives the equation $T - 10g\sin(30°) = 0$ (the body is stationary so acceleration is zero.)

Hence $T - 10g \times 0.5 = 5g(= 49)$.

Solutions: B5

Question 181 B

$$\begin{aligned} a+2b-c &= (1+i)+2(2-3i)-(-i) \\ &= 1+i+4-6i+i \\ &= 5-4i \end{aligned}$$

Question 182 C

$$\begin{aligned} b^2 &= (2-3i)^2 \\ &= 4-12i+(3i)^2 \\ &= 4-12i-9 \\ &= -5-12i \end{aligned}$$

Question 183 E

$$\begin{aligned} abc &= (1+i)(2-3i)(-i) \\ &= (1+i)(-2i+3i^2) \\ &= (1+i)(-2i-3) \\ &= -2i-3-2i^2-3i \\ &= -2i-3+2-3i \\ &= -1-5i \end{aligned}$$

(Note: A CAS could be used to check your by-hand answers.)

Question 184 C

$$\begin{aligned} z^2-4z+8 &= z^2-4z+4+4 \\ &= (z-2)^2+4 \\ &= (z-2)^2-(2i^2) \\ &= (z-2+2i)(z-2-2i) \end{aligned}$$

(Alternative **A** might look to be correct, but it is actually a set of 4 factors, the square of the answer!)

Question 185 D

Define $z=a+bi$ on a CAS and calculate $z+\dfrac{1}{z}$.

The imaginary part is $b-\dfrac{b}{a^2+b^2}$.

For the result to be real, the imaginary part must be zero.

So:

$$\begin{aligned} b-\frac{b}{a^2+b^2} &= 0 \\ 1-\frac{1}{a^2+b^2} &= 0 \quad (b \neq 0) \\ a^2+b^2 &= 1 \end{aligned}$$

This is equivalent to $|z|=1$.

(Alternatively, $z+\dfrac{1}{z}=z+\dfrac{\bar{z}}{z\bar{z}}$ which is real if $z\bar{z}=1 \Leftrightarrow a^2+b^2=1 \Leftrightarrow |z|=1$.)

Question 186 C

$i^{1!}=i^1=i;\ i^{2!}=i^2=-1$

$i^{3!}=i^6=\left(i^2\right)^3=(-1)^3=-1$

$i^{4!}=i^{24}=\left(i^4\right)^6=(1)^6=1$

The remaining 96 powers of i are of the form $4k$ for some integer k so each equals 1.

So after the first three terms, the remaining 97 terms each equal 1.

$$\begin{aligned} i^{1!}+i^{2!}+i^{3!}+\ldots+i^{100!} &= i-1-1+\ldots+1 \\ &= i-2+97 \\ &= 95+i \end{aligned}$$

(Alternatively, the 'sum' command of a CAS gives the result directly.)

Question 187 A

$$\begin{aligned} \frac{4z\bar{z}}{(z+\bar{z})^2} &= \frac{4(a+bi)(a-bi)}{(a+bi+a-bi)^2} \\ &= \frac{4\left(a^2+b^2\right)}{4a^2} \\ &= \frac{a^2+b^2}{a^2} \\ &= 1+\frac{b^2}{a^2} \end{aligned}$$

Alternative **A** has this form.

(Alternatively, using a CAS with $z=a+bi$, test each option by entering each in turn and seeing whether the output 'true' is obtained.

A CAS gives output 'true' for alternative **A**.)

Question 188 A

$$\begin{aligned} y-ix &= -i^2y-ix \text{ (as } -i^2=1) \\ &= -i(x+iy) \end{aligned}$$

$$\begin{aligned} (y-ix)^{14} &= \left(-i(x+iy)\right)^{14} \\ &= (-i)^{14}(x+iy)^{14} \\ &= \left((-i)^2\right)^7(a+ib) \\ &= (-1)^7(a+ib) \\ &= -a-ib \end{aligned}$$

Question 189 B

$z^2=(-2i)^2=4i^2=-4$

So $\left|z^2\right|=4$ and $\operatorname{Arg}\left(z^2\right)=\pi$, since $-\pi<\operatorname{Arg}\leq\pi$.

Question 190 C

$$\frac{z}{v}=\frac{3\operatorname{cis}\left(\frac{\pi}{3}\right)}{\operatorname{cis}\left(\frac{\pi}{4}\right)}$$
$$=3\operatorname{cis}\left(\frac{\pi}{3}-\frac{\pi}{4}\right)$$
$$=3\operatorname{cis}\left(\frac{4\pi-3\pi}{12}\right)$$
$$=3\operatorname{cis}\left(\frac{\pi}{12}\right)$$

Question 191 E

$$w^7=\left(2\operatorname{cis}\left(\frac{\pi}{6}\right)\right)^7$$
$$=2^7\operatorname{cis}\left(\frac{7\pi}{6}\right)$$
$$=128\operatorname{cis}\left(\frac{7\pi}{6}\right)$$

Unfortunately, this is not one of the answers.

However, $\frac{7\pi}{6}-2\pi=-\frac{5\pi}{6}$, so $\frac{7\pi}{6}$ is the same polar angle on the Argand plane as $-\frac{5\pi}{6}$.

So $w^7=128\operatorname{cis}\left(-\frac{5\pi}{6}\right)$.

Question 192 B

$$w^2v=\left(2\operatorname{cis}\left(\frac{\pi}{6}\right)\right)^2\operatorname{cis}\left(\frac{\pi}{4}\right)$$
$$=4\operatorname{cis}\left(\frac{2\pi}{6}\right)\operatorname{cis}\left(\frac{\pi}{4}\right)$$
$$=4\operatorname{cis}\left(\frac{2\pi}{6}+\frac{\pi}{4}\right)$$
$$=4\operatorname{cis}\left(\frac{4\pi+3\pi}{12}\right)$$
$$=4\operatorname{cis}\left(\frac{7\pi}{12}\right)$$

Question 193 A

Let $z=x+yi$ where $y=\operatorname{Im}(z)>0$.

$$\frac{z\bar{z}}{z-\bar{z}}=\frac{(x+yi)(x-yi)}{(x+yi)-(x-yi)}$$
$$=\frac{x^2+y^2}{2yi}$$
$$=-\frac{x^2+y^2}{2y}i\quad\left(\text{as }\frac{1}{i}=-i\right)$$
$$=-ki$$

where $k>0$ as $\frac{x^2+y^2}{2y}>0$.

$$\operatorname{Arg}(-ki)=-\frac{\pi}{2}$$
$$\operatorname{Arg}\left(\frac{z\bar{z}}{z-\bar{z}}\right)=-\frac{\pi}{2}$$

(The above calculations can be automated with a CAS.)

Question 194 C

The four points O, z, iz and $z+iz$ form the vertices of a square (the effect of multiplication by i is a $90°$ anticlockwise rotation about O).

The area of the square is $|z|^2$ so the triangle is half of this, that is $\frac{|z|^2}{2}$.

Question 195 D

The cartesian equation of the first ray is $y=x-2,\ x>2$.

The cartesian equation of the second ray is:

$$y-1=\tan\left(\frac{5\pi}{6}\right)(x-5)$$
$$=-\frac{1}{\sqrt{3}}(x-5),\ x<5$$

From the first equation, $x=y+2$.

Substituting in the second equation:

$$y-1=-\frac{1}{\sqrt{3}}(y-3)$$
$$\sqrt{3}y-\sqrt{3}=-y+3$$
$$\sqrt{3}y+y=3+\sqrt{3}$$
$$\left(\sqrt{3}+1\right)y=\sqrt{3}\left(\sqrt{3}+1\right)$$
$$y=\sqrt{3}$$

(Alternatively solve simultaneously with a CAS.)

Question 196 D

Method 1: A geometric approach

Consider a circle $|z|=r$ with centre O and radius r.

Let P be a point on the circle $|z|=r$ that touches the circle $\left|z-2-\sqrt{3}i\right|=1$.

For P to be a maximum distance from O, line segment OP must pass through $\left(2,\sqrt{3}\right)$ (the centre of the given circle).

To find the maximum value of $|z|$, find the distance from O to $\left(2,\sqrt{3}\right)$ using Pythagoras's theorem and then add 1 (the radius of the given circle).

Hence the maximum value of $|z|$ is

$$\sqrt{2^2+\left(\sqrt{3}\right)^2}+1=\sqrt{7}+1.$$

Method 2: A direct CAS approach

This involves the use of a function maximum command.

Let $z=\cos(\theta)+i\sin(\theta)$.

The value of θ, where $\theta\in[0,2\pi]$, for which $\left|\cos(\theta)+i\sin(\theta)-2-\sqrt{3}i\right|$ is a maximum is

$\theta=\tan^{-1}\left(\frac{\sqrt{3}}{2}\right)+\pi$.

Substituting this value into $\left|\cos(\theta)+i\sin(\theta)-2-\sqrt{3}i\right|$ gives $\sqrt{7}+1$.

Question 197

a. $z^2+2z+2=0$ can be solved using the quadratic formula or by completing the square.

Here is the latter approach.

$$\begin{aligned}z^2+2z+2&=0\\ z^2+2z+1+1&=0\\ (z+1)^2-i^2&=0\\ (z+1-i)(z+1+i)&=0\end{aligned}$$

So $z=-1+i,-1-i$.

b. For $z^2+2\overline{z}+2=0$, let $z=x+yi$ where x and y are real and find the values of x and y.

$$\begin{aligned}(x+yi)^2+2(x-yi)+2&=0\\ x^2-y^2+2xyi+2x-2yi+2&=0\\ x^2-y^2+2x+2+2(xy-y)i&=0\end{aligned}$$

Equate real and imaginary components:

$$\begin{aligned}x^2-y^2+2x+2&=0 \quad (1)\\ xy-y&=0 \quad (2)\end{aligned}$$

From (2), $y=0$ or $x=1$.

Substitute into (1) and solve.

If $y=0$, $x^2+2x+2=0$, and from part **a**. this has no real solutions.

If $x=1$, $5-y^2=0\Rightarrow y=\pm\sqrt{5}$.

So the given equation has solutions $z=1\pm\sqrt{5}i$.

Question 198

a. Completing the square gives:

$$\begin{aligned}2(z^2+2z+1)-2+5&=0\\ 2(z+1)^2&=-3\\ z+1&=\pm\sqrt{\frac{3}{2}}i\\ &=\pm\frac{\sqrt{6}}{2}i\\ z&=-1\pm\frac{\sqrt{6}}{2}i\end{aligned}$$

(Alternatively, use the quadratic formula.)

b. Refer to part **e**.

c. The circle of minimum radius must be centred on $(-1,0)$ with radius $\frac{\sqrt{6}}{2}$.

Hence $m=1$ and $n=\frac{\sqrt{6}}{2}$.

d. From part **c.**, $|z+1|=\frac{\sqrt{6}}{2}$, so

$$(x+1)^2+y^2=\left(\frac{\sqrt{6}}{2}\right)^2=\frac{3}{2}.$$

e.

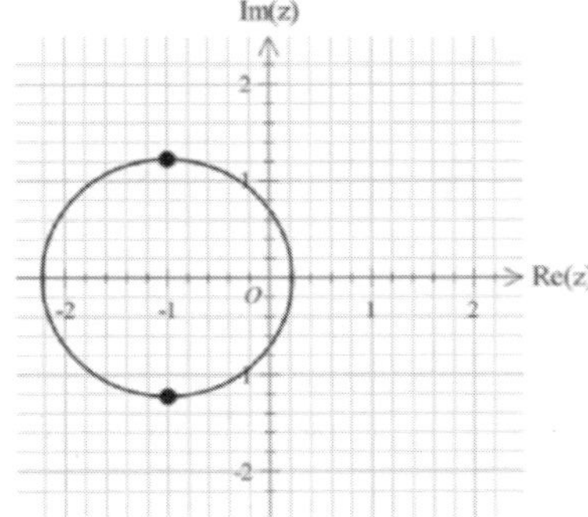

f. Solving the quadratic as in part **a.** gives

$$z+1=\pm\sqrt{\frac{2-d}{2}}.$$

(Alternatively, use the quadratic formula or the 'csolve' command of a CAS.

Using the values of m and n:

$$|z+1|\le\frac{\sqrt{6}}{2}$$
$$\left|\sqrt{\frac{2-d}{2}}\right|\le\frac{\sqrt{6}}{2}\quad *$$
$$\left|\sqrt{2-d}\right|\le\sqrt{3}$$
$$|2-d|\le 3$$
$$-1\le d\le 5$$

(A CAS can be used to solve the inequality at *.)

g. Solving the quadratic gives

$$z+\frac{b}{2a}=\pm\frac{\sqrt{b^2-4ac}}{2a}$$
$$=\pm\frac{\sqrt{4ac-b^2}}{2a}i$$

as the complex solutions have non-zero imaginary parts and so $b^2-4ac<0$.

$$\left|z+\frac{b}{2a}\right|=\left|\frac{\sqrt{4ac-b^2}}{2a}\right|$$
$$=\frac{\sqrt{4ac-b^2}}{2|a|}$$

So $p=\frac{b}{2a}$, $q=\frac{\sqrt{4ac-b^2}}{2|a|}$.

Question 199

a. With a CAS, assign/define $u=-2-i$, $v=-4-3i$ and $z=x+yi$.

Solving $|z-u|=|z-v|$ for y gives $y=-x-5$.

Alternatively, the relation $|z-u|=|z-v|$ is the perpendicular bisector of the line joining u and v.

The midpoint of u and v is:

$$\frac{u+v}{2}=\frac{(-2-i)+(-4-3i)}{2}$$
$$=-3-2i$$

The coordinates of the midpoint are $(-3,-2)$.

The gradient m of the line joining u and v is

$$m=\frac{-1-(-3)}{-2-(-4)}=1.$$

Hence the gradient of the perpendicular bisector (the required line) is -1 (since $m_1m_2=-1$ for two perpendicular lines with gradients m_1 and m_2.)

The cartesian equation of the perpendicular bisector is

$$y=-1(x-(-3))+(-2).$$

Hence $y=-x-5$.

b. See part **d**.

c. All points on the line $|z-u|=|z-v|$ are equidistant from u and v.

Equivalently, the line is the perpendicular bisector of the line joining u and v.

d. The diagram is shown below; note that the ray is open at the point $(-2,-1)$, shown by the open circle at u.

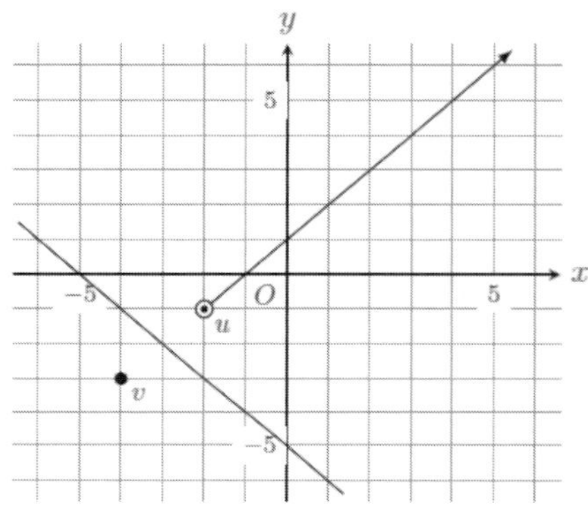

e. In cartesian form, $y=x+1$, $x>-2$.

f. $|z_c-(-5i)|=|z_c-u|=|z_c-v|=r$

Let the coordinates of z_c be (h,k).

Using u and $-5i$:

$$(-4-h)^2+(-3-k)^2=h^2+(k+5)^2 \quad (1)$$

Using v and $-5i$:

$$(-2-h)^2+(-1-k)^2=h^2+(k+5)^2 \quad (2)$$

Solving (1) and (2) simultaneously, e.g. with a CAS, gives $h=-\frac{5}{3}$ and $k=-\frac{10}{3}$.

Hence $z_c=-\frac{5}{3}-\frac{10i}{3}$.

Substituting $h=-\frac{5}{3}$ and $k=-\frac{10}{3}$ into $h^2+(k+5)^2=r^2$, for example, and solving for r with $r>0$ gives $r=\frac{5\sqrt{2}}{3}$.

Question 200

a. One approach is to find the cartesian equation of the ray $\text{Arg}(z - z_4) = \frac{5\pi}{6}$ where $z_4 = \sqrt{3} + i$.

$y - 1 = \tan\left(\frac{5\pi}{6}\right)\left(x - \sqrt{3}\right)$ where $x < \sqrt{3}$.

So $y = -\frac{1}{\sqrt{3}}x + 2,\ x < \sqrt{3}$.

(The solution can be obtained directly with a CAS.)

The ray (half-line) starts at, but does not include, $\left(\sqrt{3}, 1\right)$ denoted by an open circle).

The ray passes through $(0,2)$.

The ray is shown in part **b**.

(Alternatively, a geometric approach is to translate the ray $\text{Arg}(z) = \frac{5\pi}{6}$ by $\sqrt{3}$ units in the positive direction of the $\text{Re}(z)$ axis and 1 unit in the positive direction of the $\text{Im}(z)$ axis.)

b. The relation $|z - 3i| = 1$ is a circle with centre $(0,3)$ and radius 1.

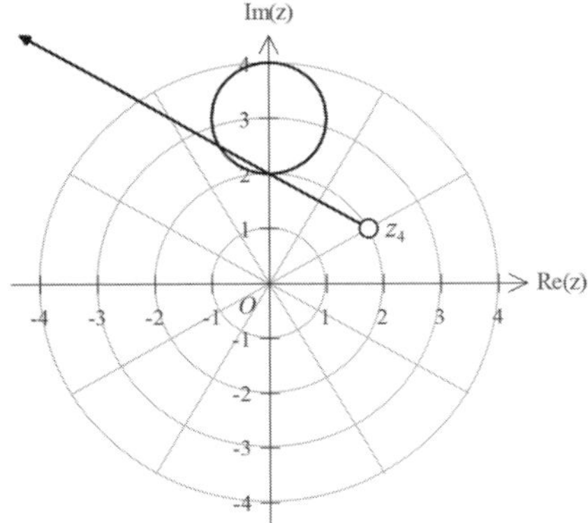

c. The radius of the circle is perpendicular to the chord and so

the angle it makes with the Im(z) axis is $\frac{\pi}{6}$.

So the minor segment formed has angle $\theta = 2\left(\frac{\pi}{6}\right) = \frac{\pi}{3}$.

Let A be the area of the minor segment.

$$A = \frac{1}{2} \times 1 \times \frac{\pi}{3} - \frac{1}{2} \times 1 \times \sin\left(\frac{\pi}{3}\right)$$

$$= \frac{\pi}{6} - \frac{\sqrt{3}}{4}$$

Solutions: B6

Question 201 D

The repeated factor in the denominator must be re-expressed as the sum of two fractions like the second two terms in alternatives **D** and **E**.

The quadratic factor in the denominator must be re-expressed as a fraction with a linear term in the numerator like the last term in alternatives **C** and **D**.

Taken together, this means that alternative **D** is correct.

(Alternatively, a CAS 'expand' command can be used to express this algebraic fraction in partial fraction form.)

Question 202 D

As sec is the reciprocal of cos, the function is undefined if $\cos\left(x+\frac{\pi}{4}\right)=0$.

Solve (with or without a CAS):

$$\cos\left(x+\frac{\pi}{4}\right)=0$$

$$x+\frac{\pi}{4}=\frac{(2n+1)\pi}{2},\ n\in Z$$

$$x=\frac{(4n+1)\pi}{4},\ n\in Z$$

Hence $x\neq\frac{(4n+1)\pi}{4}$, $n\in Z$ and the implied domain is $R\backslash\left\{\frac{(4n+1)\pi}{4}\right\}$, $n\in Z$.

(Alternatively, some CAS have a 'domain' command; one such CAS gives $x\neq\frac{(4n-3)\pi}{4}$ directly, which is equivalent to the form above.

Question 203 C

$2x-1$ must be within the domain of the arcsin function, i.e. $[-1,1]$.

Thus $-1\le 2x-1\le 1\Leftrightarrow 0\le 2x\le 2\Leftrightarrow 0\le x\le 1$.

So the domain is $[0,1]$.

(A CAS plot shows this immediately.)

Question 204 E

Range of $y=\tan^{-1}(x)$ is $\left(-\frac{\pi}{2},\frac{\pi}{2}\right)$ and its asymptotes have equations $y=\pm\frac{\pi}{2}$.

Range of $y=\frac{1}{2}\tan^{-1}(x)$ is $\left(-\frac{\pi}{4},\frac{\pi}{4}\right)$ and its asymptotes have equations $y=\pm\frac{\pi}{4}$.

(Alternatively, use a CAS to plot the graph – it is easy to see from the graph with a suitable window that only alternative **E** is correct.

Question 205 B

If $AP=BP$, then the locus is the perpendicular bisector of the line through A and B.

To find the equation of the perpendicular bisector, you need its gradient and a point through which it passes. Hence:

$$m_{AB}=\frac{-3-1}{0-(-2)}=-2$$

$$m_{\perp}=\frac{1}{2}$$

$$\text{midpt } AB=(-1,-1)$$

So the equation of the locus is:

$$y+1=\frac{1}{2}(x+1)\Leftrightarrow x-2y=1$$

(Alternatively, find algebraic expressions for AP and BP, equate them and simplify.)

Question 206 E

The distance of P from $(0,-a)$ is given by $\sqrt{(x-0)^2+(y-(-a))^2}=\sqrt{x^2+(y+a)^2}$.

The distance of P from $y=a$ is given by $|y-a|$.

Square, equate and simplify:

$$x^2+(y+a)^2=(y-a)^2$$

$$x^2+y^2+2ay+a^2=y^2-2ay+a^2$$

$$x^2=-4ay$$

$$y=-\frac{1}{4a}x^2$$

Question 207 A

The equation can be re-expressed as

$$2x^2+4y^2=1\Leftrightarrow\frac{x^2}{\left(\frac{1}{2}\right)}+\frac{y^2}{\left(\frac{1}{4}\right)}=1$$

which is of the form $\frac{x^2}{a^2}+\frac{y^2}{b^2}=1$, the general form of the equation of an ellipse.

Question 208 D

Adding the equations gives $x+y=2$, which can be re-expressed in the form $y=-x+2$.

Question 209 E

The graph with equation $\frac{x^2}{9}-y^2=1$ is of the form $\frac{x^2}{a^2}-\frac{y^2}{b^2}=1$, so it is a hyperbola.

The equations of its asymptotes are $y=\pm\frac{bx}{a}$.

Here, $a=3$ and $b=1$ so the asymptotes are given by $y=\pm\frac{x}{3}$.

Question 210 A

First find r:

$$r=\sqrt{x^2+y^2}=\sqrt{\left(\sqrt{3}\right)^2+(-1)^2}=2$$

Next find θ:

$$\tan(\theta)=\frac{y}{x}=-\frac{1}{\sqrt{3}}$$

As $\left(\sqrt{3},-1\right)$ is in the fourth quadrant, $\theta=-30°$ and the polar form is $[2,-30°]$.

Question 211 B

For $[3,120°]$, $r=3$ and $\theta=120°$.

$$x=r\cos(\theta)=3\times\left(-\frac{1}{2}\right)=-\frac{3}{2}$$
$$y=r\sin(\theta)=3\times\left(\frac{\sqrt{3}}{2}\right)=\frac{3\sqrt{3}}{2}$$

Thus $[3,120°]$ becomes $\left(-\frac{3}{2},\frac{3\sqrt{3}}{2}\right)$.

Question 212 C

To convert r to positive 2, add $180°$ to the given angle, giving polar coordinates $[2,160°]$.

Question 213 B

$$r=\frac{1}{1-\sin(\theta)}$$
$$r(1-\sin(\theta))=1$$
$$r-r\sin(\theta)=1$$
$$r-y=1 \text{ (since } y=r\sin(\theta))$$
$$r=y+1$$
$$r^2=y^2+2y+1$$

But $r^2=x^2+y^2$, so

$$x^2+y^2=y^2+2y+1$$
$$x^2=2y+1$$
$$2y=x^2-1$$
$$y=\frac{1}{2}(x^2-1)$$

Question 214 B

$$2r\sin(\theta)=r^2-1$$

Now, since $y=r\sin(\theta)$

$$2y=r^2-1$$

And since $r^2=x^2+y^2$

$$2y=x^2+y^2-1$$
$$x^2=y^2-2y-1$$

Now complete the square:

$$x^2+y^2-2y+1-1=1$$
$$x^2+(y-1)^2=2$$

Question 215 A

$$2x^2+2y^2=32$$

Divide by 2:

$$x^2+y^2=16$$

And since $r^2=x^2+y^2$

$r^2=16$, so $r=\pm4$.

But as the circle with equation $r=-4$ is identical in appearance to the circle with equation $r=4$, only one equation is needed.

Question 216 E

The graph is that of $y=-k|x|$ translated 2 units left and 3 units up, and k must be $\frac{2}{3}$ or $\frac{3}{2}$ from the alternatives.

Alternatives **C** (as $|x+2|=|2+x|$) and **E** give correct translations, but **C** has the wrong sign.

It is easy to check graphically that alternative **E** gives the correct x-intercepts.

Question 217 A

Use the formula $\cot^2(t)+1=\operatorname{cosec}^2(t)$.

$$\cot(t)=\frac{y+1}{3};\ \operatorname{cosec}(t)=\frac{x-1}{2}$$

$$\left(\frac{y+1}{3}\right)^2+1=\left(\frac{x-1}{2}\right)^2$$

$$\frac{(x-1)^2}{4}-\frac{(y+1)^2}{9}=1$$

Question 218 E

Recall that one parametric form uses the formula $\cos^2+\sin^2=1$ so check alternatives **C**, **D** and **E**.

It is easy to see that alternative **C** gives $\text{LHS}=9\cos^2(t)+4\sin^2(t)\neq 1$ while alternative **D** has the 2s and 3s mixed up.

Alternative **E** works.

(Alternative **A** gives half of the ellipse, while alternative **B** is the parametric form for a hyperbola.)

Question 219

Any points with negative r values should be converted to points with positive r values first.

You do this by adding π to the angle.

You could change $-\frac{5\pi}{4}$ into $\frac{3\pi}{4}$ but this is not particularly useful.

The new list looks like this:

$A\left[1,\frac{\pi}{4}\right]$, $B\left[2,\frac{5\pi}{4}\right]$, $C\left[3,\frac{3\pi}{4}\right]$, $D\left[2,-\frac{5\pi}{4}\right]$

Here is a plot of these points.

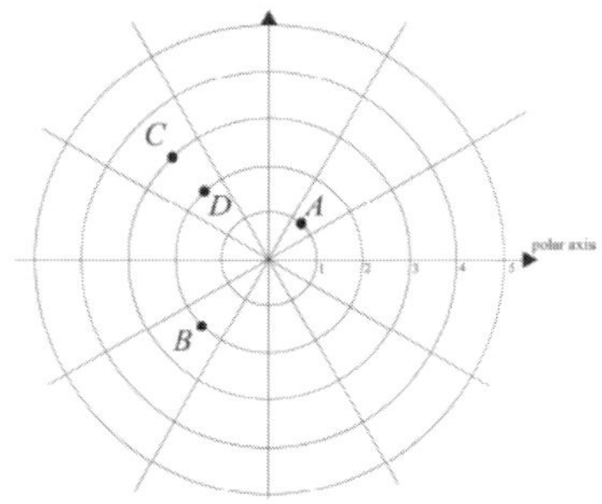

Question 220

a. Completing this table using values correct to 2 decimal places gives this:

θ	0	$\frac{\pi}{6}$	$\frac{\pi}{3}$	$\frac{\pi}{2}$	$\frac{2\pi}{3}$
r	1	2	7.46	∞	7.46

θ	π	$\frac{4\pi}{3}$	$\frac{3\pi}{2}$	$\frac{5\pi}{3}$	2π
r	1	0.54	0.5	0.54	1

b. Plotting the graph from the table is a little awkward at the points where $\theta=\frac{2\pi}{3}$ and $\theta=\pi$.

It is possible that some more points may be needed.

The final graph is a parabola as shown.

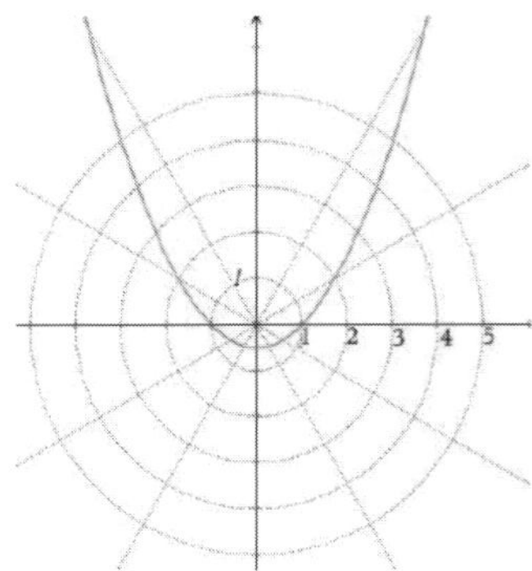

Question 221

The graph with equation $y^2=4(x+4)$ is a translation left by 4 units of the graph with equation $y^2=4x$ (a 'side parabola').

$x=0$: $y^2=16$ giving $y=\pm 4$

The y-intercept is $(-4,0)$ and this is the vertex of the parabola. Here is its graph.

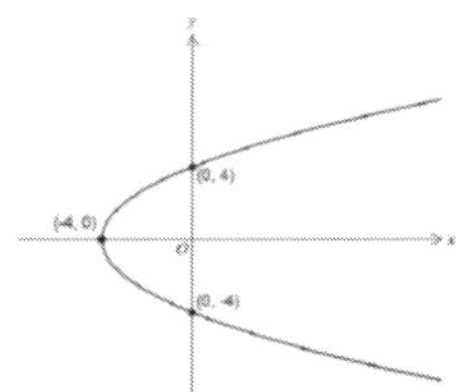

Question 222

Substitute $y=x-2$ into the ellipse equation:

$$\frac{(x-2)^2}{4}+(x-2+1)^2=1$$
$$(x-2)^2+4(x-1)^2=4$$
$$x^2-4x+4+4x^2-8x+4=4$$
$$5x^2-12x+4=0$$
$$(5x-2)(x-2)=0$$

$x=\frac{2}{5}\Rightarrow y=-\frac{8}{5}$ or $x=2\Rightarrow y=0$

So the coordinates are $\left(\frac{2}{5},-\frac{8}{5}\right)$ and $(-2,0)$.

Question 223

a. $x=\sqrt{t-2} \Rightarrow x^2=t-2 \Leftrightarrow t=x^2+2$

Substitute for t in the equation for y:

$y=2t=2x^2+4$

b. $2 \le t \le 6$, so $0 \le x \le 2$

Thus the graph is part of a parabola (not the complete parabola).

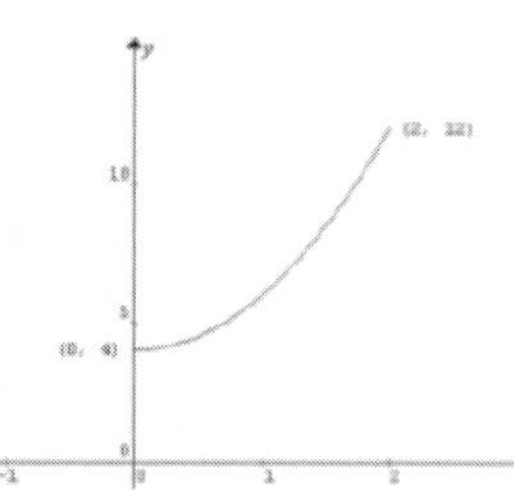

Question 224

$$\frac{3x}{(2-x)(4+x^2)}=\frac{A}{2-x}+\frac{Bx+C}{4+x^2}$$

$$3x=A(4+x^2)+(Bx+C)(2-x)$$

$x=2 \Rightarrow 6=8A$ and so $A=\frac{3}{4}$.

Considering the coefficients of x^2:

$$0=A-B \Rightarrow B=\frac{3}{4}$$

Considering the constant terms:

$$0=4A+2C \Rightarrow C=-\frac{3}{2}$$

So $\dfrac{3x}{(2-x)(4+x^2)}=\dfrac{3}{4(2-x)}+\dfrac{3x}{4(4+x^2)}-\dfrac{3}{2(4+x^2)}$.

(Alternatively, a CAS 'expand' command can be used to express this algebraic fraction in partial fraction form.)

Question 225

Vertical asymptotes occur when $\cos(4x)=0$.

$x \in \left[-\frac{\pi}{4},\frac{\pi}{4}\right]$ and so $4x \in [-\pi,\pi]$

$$4x=-\frac{\pi}{2},\frac{\pi}{2}$$

$$x=-\frac{\pi}{8},\frac{\pi}{8}$$

Endpoint coordinates:

$$\sec\left(4\left(\pm\frac{\pi}{4}\right)\right)=\sec(\pm\pi)$$

$$=\frac{1}{\cos(\pm\pi)}$$

$$=-1$$

The turning point is located at $(0,1)$.

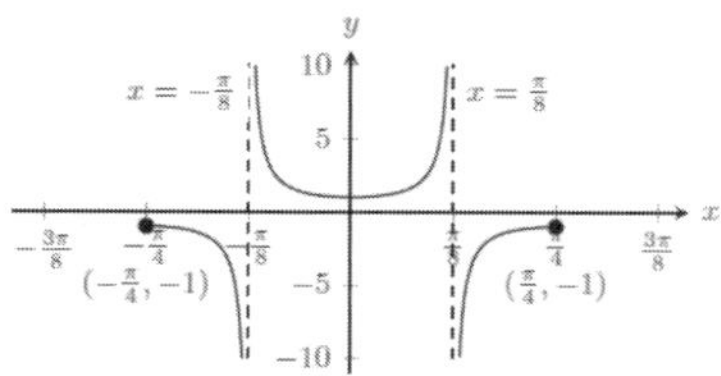

Notes

Notes

Notes

Notes

Notes

Notes

Notes

Notes

Notes